Renewable
Electricity Generation

Renewable
Electricity Generation

Economic Analysis and Outlook

Benjamin Zycher

The AEI Press

Publisher for the American Enterprise Institute

WASHINGTON, D.C.

Distributed by arrangement with the Rowman & Littlefield Publishing Group, 4501 Forbes Boulevard, Suite 200, Lanham, Maryland 20706. To order, call toll free 1-800-462-6420 or 1-717-794-3800. For all other inquiries, please contact AEI Press, 1150 Seventeenth Street, N.W., Washington, D.C. 20036, or call 1-800-862-5801.

Library of Congress Cataloging-in-Publication Data

Zycher, Benjamin.
  Renewable electricity generation : economic analysis and outlook /
Benjamin Zycher.
      p. cm.
  Includes bibliographical references and index.
  ISBN-13: 978-0-8447-7221-9 (cloth : alk. paper)
  ISBN-10: 0-8447-7221-6 (cloth : alk. paper)
  ISBN-13: 978-0-8447-7222-6 (pbk. : alk. paper)
  ISBN-10: 0-8447-7222-4 (pbk. : alk. paper)
  [etc.]
  1. Renewable energy sources—Economic aspects—United States.
  2. Electric power production—United States. I. Title.
  TJ807.9.U5Z93 2011
  333.79'4—dc23

                                                    2011032424

© 2011 by the American Enterprise Institute for Public Policy Research, Washington, D.C. All rights reserved. No part of this publication may be used or reproduced in any manner whatsoever without permission in writing from the American Enterprise Institute except in the case of brief quotations embodied in news articles, critical articles, or reviews. The views expressed in the publications of the American Enterprise Institute are those of the authors and do not necessarily reflect the views of the staff, advisory panels, officers, or trustees of AEI.

Printed in the United States of America

Contents

List of Illustrations

Acknowledgments

Sincere thanks are due the National Research Initiative program at the American Enterprise Institute (AEI) for generous financial support of this work; but the views expressed are the author's alone and do not purport to represent those of AEI or of any of its officers or sponsors. Great appreciation is due as well to Gary B. Ackerman, Wayne T. Brough, Christopher DeMuth, Laurence Dougharty, Kenneth P. Green, Peter Z. Grossman, Larry D. Hamlin, Steven F. Hayward, Steven A. Huhman, Cotton M. Lindsay, Robert J. Michaels, Henry Olsen, Jerry Taylor, and Thomas P. Treat for useful suggestions. The author is responsible for any remaining errors.

Executive Summary

This book examines the outlook for renewable energy in electricity generation as a substitute for such conventional fuels as coal and natural gas. The emphasis is on wind power, which, in terms of projected generation capacity, is by far the most important of the non-hydroelectric forms of renewable power. Some analysis of solar energy is presented also. The discussion examines as well the central arguments in favor of policies supporting the expanded use of renewables, and the implications of prospective supply and price developments in the market for natural gas.

Public policy support for renewable electricity is substantial. This support takes the form of direct and indirect subsidies, and requirements in a majority of the states that specific percentages of the market for electric power be reserved for electricity produced from renewable sources. Nonetheless, renewable power provides only a small proportion of electric power in the United States, and official projections are for slow growth at most. This market resistance to investment in renewable generation capacity can be explained by the problems intrinsic to renewable power—that is, the inherent limitations on its competitiveness—that public policies can circumvent or neutralize only at very substantial expense. These problems uniformly yield high costs and low reliability for renewable power, and can be summarized as follows:

- The unconcentrated energy content of renewable-energy sources

- Location (or siting) limitations

- Relatively low availability ("capacity factors") over time combined with the intermittent nature of wind flows and sunlight.

The low energy content of sunlight and wind flows relative to that of fossil or nuclear fuels forces renewable technology to compensate by relying upon massive substitute investment in land and/or materials. Second, unlike conventional generation technologies, renewable generation is sharply constrained by siting problems because favorable sunlight and wind conditions are limited geographically, yielding additional costs for transmission. Finally, capacity factors—essentially, the portion of the year during which renewable facilities can actually generate power—are substantially lower for wind and solar facilities than for most conventional generation, and the intermittent nature of sunlight and wind flows exacerbates this problem. These conditions result in a need for conventional backup generation capacity so as to preserve the stability of the electric grid and prevent power shortages; this increases associated costs substantially. Moreover, for wind power in particular, actual power generation tends to be concentrated in off-peak periods—winds tend to blow at night and in the winter—so that the electricity produced from wind facilities tends to be less valuable than that produced from conventional sources.

The five central rationales commonly offered in support of subsidies and mandates for renewables can be summarized as follows:

- **The "infant-industry" argument:** Renewables cannot compete with conventional electric generation technologies on an equal basis because scale and learning efficiencies can be achieved only with an expanded market share.

- **The "level-playing-field" argument:** Subsidies enjoyed by conventional technologies introduce an artificial competitive disadvantage for renewable technologies.

- **A second "level-playing-field" argument:** The adverse environmental effects (e.g., air pollution) of conventional electricity generation create an additional artificial cost advantage for those technologies.

- **The resource-depletion (or "sustainability") argument:** Policy support for renewables is justified as a tool with which to slow the depletion of such conventional resources as natural gas and to hasten the development of technologies providing alternatives for future generations.

- **The "green-employment" argument:** Policy support for renewables will yield expanded employment (and economic competitiveness).

These rationales are deeply problematic. The infant-industry argument is inconsistent with the cost evidence for renewables and with the presence of an international capital market. The subsidies per kilowatt-hour enjoyed by renewables outweigh by far those bestowed upon conventional generation technologies, so that the first level-playing-field argument is unsupported by the evidence. With respect to the adverse environmental effects of conventional generation, the cost of conventional backup capacity made necessary by the unreliability of wind and solar generation is substantially greater than any artificial cost advantage enjoyed by conventional technologies as a result of negative external effects assumed not to have been corrected ("internalized") by current policies. The resource-depletion or sustainability criticism of conventional technologies is incorrect simply as a matter of basic economics, and is inconsistent with the historical evidence. Finally, the premise that expansion of renewable power will yield an increase in "green employment" confuses benefits for a particular group with costs imposed upon the economy as a whole, and fails to distinguish between employment growth in the aggregate and employment shifts among economic sectors. In short, the purported social benefits of policy support for renewables are illusory.

The market difficulties faced by renewables are likely to be exacerbated by ongoing supply and price developments in the market for natural gas, which will weaken further the competitive position of renewable power generation. At the same time, subsidies and mandates for renewables impose nontrivial costs upon taxpayers and consumers in electricity markets. The upshot is the imposition of substantial net burdens upon the U.S. economy as a whole, even as the policies bestow important benefits upon particular groups and industries, thus yielding enhanced incentives for innumerable interests to seek favors from government. As is the case in most contexts, the resource uses emerging from market competition, even as constrained and distorted by tax and regulatory policies, are the best guides for the achievement of resource allocation that is most productive. As federal and state policymakers address the ongoing issues and problems afflicting renewable electricity generation, the realities of this recent history provide a useful guide for policy reform.

Introduction

This study examines the outlook for renewable energy in electricity generation as a substitute for such conventional fuels as coal and natural gas; the emphasis is on wind power, which in terms of projected generation capacity is by far the most important of the non-hydroelectric forms of renewable power, with some discussion of solar energy.[1] The discussion examines as well the central arguments in favor of policies supporting the expanded use of renewables and the implications of prospective supply and price developments in the market for natural gas.

Renewable energy has no uniform definition, but the essential characteristic of most taxonomies is natural replenishment of the given energy resource; this is a sharp descriptive distinction from conventional energy sources, which by assumption are fixed in terms of the total physical quantities in existence.[2] Accordingly, consumption of one unit (for example, a

---

[1] The U.S. Energy Information Administration (EIA) projects that in 2035 generation capacity from renewables will be about 149 GW (gigawatts), of which about 80 GW will be conventional hydropower, about 55 GW will be wind generation capacity, and about 1.9 GW will be solar capacity. See EIA, at http://www.eia.gov/oiaf/aeo/tablebrowser/#release=AEO2011&subject=0AEO2011&table=16-AEO2011&region=0-0&cases=ref2011-d020911a. Note that a year earlier the EIA projection for 2035 was about 209 GW of total renewables capacity, with the respective shares projected to be about 78 GW, 71 GW, and 14.6 GW. See EIA, at http://www.eia.doe.gov/oiaf/archive/aeo10/aeoref_tab.html, at table 16. Putting aside issues of reliability and availability, a gigawatt of capacity is enough to serve, very roughly, 750,000 to 1,000,000 homes, but that rule of thumb, while crudely appropriate for conventional generation capacity, may not reflect the reliability and availability issues afflicting renewables. This is discussed further in chapter 2. See also fn. 16 below.

[2] Note that other inputs used as complements with the energy content of wind flows and sunlight still are subject to the same physical-scarcity problem characterizing conventional fuels. Good examples are the land needed for wind farms and solar-thermal energy facilities and the "rare earth" minerals needed for some components of wind turbines, solar photovoltaic cells, and other renewable energy technologies. Examples of these rare-earth minerals are dysprosium, neodymium, praseodymium, and samarium, used for the magnets in wind turbines. For a discussion of rare earth minerals, see the U.S. Department of Energy, at http://www.energy.gov/news/documents/criticalmaterialsstrategy.pdf. Moreover, the general economic scarcity condition still applies fully to renewable energy sources:

cubic foot of natural gas) automatically reduces the physical supply of that resource by that one unit.[3] As discussed in chapter 3, there actually is no analytic (or economic) difference between renewable and nonrenewable resources in this replenishment (*or sustainability*) context, a point that may seem counterintuitive at first glance. In any event, the Environmental Protection Agency (EPA) maintains a list of the energy forms that qualify as renewable under the various definitions imposed by the states that require or have goals for the use of renewable energy in electricity generation.[4]

The outlook for renewable energy in electricity generation is an issue of considerable importance, as there exists substantial political support for government policies promoting a sharp expansion in the absolute and relative role of renewables. One prominent example is provided by President Barack Obama, who argued as follows in June of 2010:

> Each of us has a part to play in a new future that will benefit all of us. As we recover from this recession, the transition to clean energy has the potential to grow our economy and create millions of jobs—but only if we accelerate that transition. Only if we seize the moment. And only if we rally together and act as one nation—workers and entrepreneurs; scientists and citizens; the public and private sectors.[5]

---

there is only so much energy content in a given wind speed/time dynamic or a given intensity of sunlight or a given volume of, say, biomass material. Moreover, that energy content can vary greatly in terms of availability over time. Some implications of this problem of economic scarcity are explored further in chapter 3.

[3] The Environmental Protection Agency lists five non-hydroelectric energy sources for electricity generation as renewable: solar, geothermal, biomass, landfill gas, and wind. See http://www.epa.gov/cleanenergy/energy-and-you/affect/non-hydro.html. Solar power takes two forms: Photovoltaic solar energy is produced when sunlight heats a surface coating in a solar panel, which then reacts with an underlying material, producing an electric current. With respect to solar-thermal generation, there are, as a rough generalization, three basic technologies in use: trough systems, solar towers, and parabolic dishes (the most common). Each uses sunlight to heat water or some other liquid or material, either directly or through the use of mirrors, producing heat with which steam is produced to turn a generator. Biomass power is electricity produced from the residues of timber and lumber production, waste paper, the waste products of commercial crop production—cornstalks are a good example—tires, municipal solid waste, and other waste products.

[4] See the EPA compilation of technologies eligible under the respective state rules at http://www.epa.gov/chp/state-policy/renewable_fs.html. Thirty states have such requirements, while an additional seven have nonmandatory goals for the use of renewable energy in electricity generation. Table 5 in the appendix to chapter 1 summarizes these data.

[5] See http://www.whitehouse.gov/issues/energy-and-environment, quoted June 15, 2010.

President Obama again:

> We can remain one of the world's leading importers of foreign oil, or we can make the investments that would allow us to become the world's leading exporter of renewable energy. We can let climate change continue to go unchecked, or we can help stop it. We can let the jobs of tomorrow be created abroad, or we can create those jobs right here in America and lay the foundation for lasting prosperity.[6]

That this political support is substantially bipartisan is illustrated by this passage from the State of the Union address in 2007. President George W. Bush said, "It's in our vital interest to diversify America's energy supply, and the way forward is through technology. We must continue changing the way America generates electric power by even greater use of clean-coal technology; solar and wind energy; and clean, safe nuclear power."[7]

Perhaps a bit more specifically, the EPA argues that "clean energy offers a cost-effective way to meet our nation's growing demand for electricity and natural gas while reducing emissions of air pollutants and greenhouse gases, lowering energy costs, and improving the reliability and security of the energy system."[8] These themes are found again in a recent report from the American Council on Renewable Energy: "America needs energy that is secure, reliable, improves public health, protects the environment, addresses climate change, creates jobs, and provides technological leadership.... America will need coordinated, sustained federal and state policies that expand renewable energy markets."[9]

This political support is reflected in current legal and regulatory requirements—mandates or standards—in many states for the use of renewable energy sources for given percentages of the respective states' electricity generation, consumption, or sales in the context of some timetable. Moreover, at both the federal and state levels, investment in and production of renewable electricity receive important subsidies, which take the form of

---

[6] See http://www.whitehouse.gov/issues/energy-and-environment, quoted March 19, 2009.
[7] See http://www.washingtonpost.com/wp-dyn/content/article/2007/01/23/AR2007012301075.html.
[8] See http://www.epa.gov/statelocalclimate/documents/pdf/guide_action_full.pdf, at ES-1.
[9] See http://www.acore.org/files/RECAP/docs/JointOutlookReport2007.pdf

direct payments to producers and such support as the federal production tax credit for power generated by wind and other renewable technologies.[10]

As discussed in chapter 1, public policy support for renewable electricity technologies began no later than the 1970s. Nonetheless, net electricity generation from all renewable sources (other than hydroelectric) was only 3.6 percent of total U.S. net generation in 2009, an increase from 2.2 percent in 1996.[11] Recent estimates[12] from the U.S. Energy Information Administration (EIA) project an increase in that proportion to about 9 percent in 2020 and 11 percent in 2030; but as recently as 2007 the EIA projected that non-hydroelectric renewable electricity generation would be only 3.6 percent of the total in 2030, the same proportion as in 2009.[13] The absence of major recent technological or cost shifts favoring renewable generation suggests that this sudden increase may be more political than economic in origin.

There has been an expansion in recent years of federal subsidies for renewable-electricity investment and production; moreover, as noted above, many states have implemented requirements for an increasing market share for renewable energy in their respective electric-generation mixes. These requirements are called *renewable portfolio standards* (RPS).[14]

---

[10] Depending on the particular technology, the production tax credit is either 2.2 cents or 1.1 cents per kilowatt-hour (kWh). Various other indirect subsidies are offered by the federal government, and state governments offer a broad array of indirect subsidies as well. See the various summaries provided by the Database of State Incentives for Renewables and Efficiency, at http://www.dsireusa.org/.

[11] See the data reported by the U.S. Energy Information Administration, at http:// www.eia.doe.gov/cneaf/electricity/epm/table1_1.html; see also table 1-3 below.

[12] See various tables and spreadsheets, at http://www.eia.doe.gov/fuelelectric.html and http://www.eia.doe.gov/oiaf/forecasting.html.

[13] See the U.S. Energy Information Administration, *Annual Energy Outlook 2007*, at http://tonto.eia.doe.gov/ftproot/forecasting/0383%282007%29.pdf, p. 86. See also Robert J. Michaels, "A Federal Renewable Electricity Requirement: What's Not to Like?" Cato Institute Policy Analysis No. 627, November 13, 2008, at http://www.cato.org/pub_display.php?pub_id=9768. Michaels notes that in the 2007 EIA analysis, "Only extreme changes in assumptions lead to a prediction of over 4 percent renewable power in 2030." Michaels notes as well that in the 2007 EIA projection, renewable electricity generation still would be less than 5 percent of total generation in 2030 even if all states with renewable power requirements were in full compliance.

[14] There is no similar RPS at the federal level; but the American Clean Energy and Security Act of 2009 (H.R. 2454, or "Waxman-Markey") passed the House of Representatives by a vote of 219 to 212; it contained provisions requiring electricity suppliers to meet 6 percent of their retail sales loads in 2012 with renewable energy and improved "efficiency," rising to 20 percent in 2020. Of that growing requirement, 75 percent was required to be met through the use of renewable energy. For a summary of that legislation, see http://thomas.loc.gov/ cgi-bin/bdquery/z?d111:H.R.2454:. The 2005 Energy Policy Act did impose a requirement that the federal government itself use renewable sources

For the federal government, the Energy Information Administration has estimated that the total cost of subsidies and support for all energy forms was about $8.7 billion in 1999, growing to $17.1 billion in 2007.[15] For renewable energy, the respective 1999 and 2007 figures were $1.4 billion and $5 billion. Moreover, the American Recovery and Reinvestment Act (the stimulus bill of 2009) included over $80 billion for various clean energy, energy efficiency, and technology programs and projects, of which $23 billion are to be directed toward renewable-energy development.[16] It

for 3 percent of its electricity consumption in fiscal years (FY) 2007–2009, 5 percent in FY2010–2012, and 7.5 percent thereafter. Under Executive Order 13423 (January 24, 2007) at least half of that renewable consumption must come from new renewable sources; but the mandate overall is limited by a constraint that such federal consumption of renewable energy be economically feasible and technically practical. See http://www1.eere.energy.gov/femp/technologies/ renewable_requirements.html. Note also that in his most recent State of the Union address President Obama called for "80 percent of America's electricity [to be generated by] clean energy sources." See the president's address at http://www.whitehouse.gov/the-press-office/2011/01/25/ remarks-president-state-union-address. The president defined "clean energy sources" to be "wind and solar [and] nuclear, clean coal, and natural gas." Depending upon the definition of "clean coal," the goal already may have been met. See tables 1-2 and 1-3 below, and fn. 1, supra. Energy secretary Steven Chu stated subsequently that coal gasification, oxyburning, and the installation of carbon dioxide scrubbers on existing coal-fired power plants are three options for "clean coal" power generation. See http:// www.platts.com/RSSFeedDetailedNews/RSSFeed/ElectricPower/6786337. Alternatively, "clean coal" may be defined as the combustion of pulverized coal subject to a carbon capture and sequestration process, a very expensive technology. See, for example, Stephen Ansolabehere et al., *The Future of Coal: Options for a Carbon-Constrained World*, Cambridge: MIT, 2007, at http://web.mit. edu/coal/ The_Future_of_ Coal.pdf, at table A-3.E.3.

[15] Year 2009 dollars; these figures include federal subsidies for transmission and distribution. See U.S. Energy Information Administration, "Federal Financial Interventions and Subsidies in Energy Markets 2007," April 2008, report no. SR/CNEAF/2008-01, at http://www.eia.doe.gov/oiaf/service rpt/subsidy2/index.html, at table 26; see also author computations using consumer price index data from the U.S. Department of Labor. These subsidies and support take the forms of direct expenditures to producers or consumers of energy, tax expenditures that reduce the federal tax liabilities of firms or individuals undertaking specific actions with respect to energy production or consumption, research and development outlays, and such specific electricity programs as the Tennessee Valley Authority.

[16] See "Progress Report: The Transformation to a Clean Energy Economy," a memorandum for the president, from Vice President Joe Biden, December 15, 2009, at http://www.whitehouse.gov/administration/vice-president-biden/reports/progress-report-transformation-clean-energy-economy. The vice president argues in the memorandum that by the end of 2010 "we will have made commitments to support more than 15 GW of new wind, solar and geothermal and other renewable energy—enough renewable energy to power 4–5 million homes per year." Note that this suggests that a gigawatt of renewable capacity would serve the equivalent of about three hundred thousand homes; see fn. 1, supra. An interactive feature on the website states that "the president's goal of doubling our renewable-energy generation, including solar, wind, and geothermal, will be reached in just 3 years," a projection that if realized would mean that renewable electricity generation would be about 7 percent of net generation by 2012. One problem with such projections is that the actual performance of renewable energy capacity in power delivery differs substantially from that of such conventional capacity as coal, natural gas, and nuclear generating stations, which are "dispatchable"—that is, they

is somewhat amusing that in December 2010 the Obama administration filed a complaint with the World Trade Organization over Chinese subsidies for wind-energy manufacturers.[17]

The small market share of renewable energy in electricity generation, despite the substantial policy support summarized above, suggests that there may exist some inherent set of important limitations on the competitiveness of renewable energy, which government policies cannot circumvent except at costs unacceptable to effective majority political coalitions. The fact that thirty states have found it necessary to mandate that a certain portion of their electricity output, consumption, or sales (depending on the state) come from renewable sources suggests that (regulated) market forces even combined with important subsidies are viewed as unlikely to achieve the renewables goals, at a minimum on the timetable set forth in the various state legal requirements.[18]

This paper examines the prospects for a large increase in the market share of renewables in electricity generation, with an emphasis on wind and solar technologies. The central arguments in support of policies expanding the role of renewable energy are scrutinized as well. Chapter 1 summarizes the history of public policy support for renewables and some details of current state requirements and goals in terms of the respective market shares mandated for renewable electricity. Chapter 2 discusses some important problems that afflict renewable electricity generation,

---

can begin or stop (or increase or decrease) production at the command of a grid manager, sometimes with a time lag. This is discussed in chapters 3 and 4. For a discussion of ongoing problems with implementation of these programs, see "Renewable Energy Loan Guarantees and Grants," a memorandum for the president, from Carol Browner, Ron Klain, and Larry Summers, October 25, 2010, at http://www.politico.com/static/ PPM182_101105_renewable_energy_memo.html.

[17] See http://www.businessweek.com/news/2010-12-23/obama-s-china-wind-power-complaint-backed-by-companies.html. For a brief Chinese response, see http://www.china-embassy.org/eng/zmgx/t781305.htm.

[18] On the other hand, it is possible that the mandates simply are a way to shift financing of renewables subsidies from the taxpayers writ large to the electricity market itself, as most state regulation of electricity rates bundles (or combines) lower- and higher-cost power into a single set of rates. This has the effect of subsidizing higher-cost power at the expense of producers and consumers of lower-cost power. These implicit regulatory tax/expenditure transfers do not appear in government fiscal accounts. However, the very need for such implicit but sizable subsidies, however financed, suggests, again, a fundamental competitiveness problem. Note that the latest EIA projections (discussed above) envision a market share for renewable-electricity generation markedly lower than those typically mandated in the respective state requirements. These requirements are summarized in the appendix to chapter 1.

either disproportionately relative to conventional energy or uniquely. Chapter 3 examines the central rationales often offered in favor of policy support for renewables, while chapter 4 discusses some implications of recent supply developments in the U.S. natural gas market. The last chapter offers conclusions and some implications for policy formulation.

1

A Summary of Public Policy
Support for Renewable Energy
in Electricity Generation

A brief history of U.S. energy policy, both generally and with respect to renewable and alternative sources in particular, can usefully begin in the mid-1970s with the energy "crisis" and the perceived need to achieve an expansion of the supply and "independence" of U.S. energy production.[19] This central rationale has shifted over time somewhat toward a combination of energy independence, environmental, and sustainability rationales; but the early policy history begins usefully with the dominant energy-security concerns of that period. The National Energy Act of 1978 was focused for the most part on reducing dependence on foreign oil and on measures intended to increase conservation and efficiency in domestic energy consumption. The NEA included the Public Utility Regulatory Policies Act, directed at improved conservation and efficiency in the electric-utility sector. PURPA required electric utilities to purchase electricity from "qualifying facilities," which were defined as electric-power producers smaller than 80 megawatts (MW) in capacity, using cogeneration processes or renewable

---

[19] Useful discussions are provided by the EIA, "Policies to Promote Non-hydro Renewable Energy in the United States and Selected Countries," February 2005, at www.eia.doe.gov/cneaf/solar. renewables/page/non_hydro/nonhydrorenewablespaper_final.pdf#page=1; Fredric Beck and Eric Martinot, "Renewable Energy Policies and Barriers," *Encyclopedia of Energy*, ed. Cutler J. Cleveland, vol. 5 (Amsterdam; Boston: Elsevier Academic Press, 2004), pp. 365–383; EIA, "Renewable Energy 2000: Issues and Trends," February 2001, at www.eia.gov/FTPROOT/renewables/06282000.pdf; Eric Martinot, Ryan Wiser, and Jan Hamrin, "Renewable Energy Policies and Markets in the United States," at http://www.martinot.info/Martinot_et_al_CRS.pdf, (San Francisco: Center for Resource Solutions, 2004); and the DSIRE database, op. cit., fn. 10 above.

technologies.[20] The NEA included also the 1978 Energy Tax Act, which gave an investment tax credit of 30 percent to residential consumers for solar- and wind-energy equipment and awarded a 10 percent investment tax credit to businesses installing solar-, wind-, geothermal-, and ocean-energy technologies. These tax credits ended in 1985.[21]

The 1992 Energy Policy Act created the production tax credit, set originally at 1.5 cents per kilowatt hour (kWh), adjusted for inflation. As noted above, the credit now is either 2.2 cents per kWh or 1.1 cents per kWh, depending on the particular renewable technology.[22] This credit has had a somewhat erratic history, having expired and been extended several times; the most recent extensions were in October 2008 and February 2009.[23] A number of other federal policies encourage the use of renewable energy in electricity generation. Qualified investments are eligible for accelerated depreciation and bonus depreciation under the 2008 and 2009 legislation and under the Tax Relief, Unemployment Insurance Reauthorization, and Job Creation Act of 2010. Certain rebates for renewable energy offered consumers by electric utilities are excluded from taxable income. Several other grant, subsidy, and loan programs are administered by various federal agencies.[24]

---

[20] Cogeneration facilities, now more commonly called "combined heat and power" (CHP) facilities, produce electricity and then capture the resulting heat for heating purposes. Under PURPA, utilities were required to purchase this power at "avoided cost," the determination of which was left to the state regulatory authorities; but the upshot is that higher-cost power is "bundled" with lower-cost power in the determination of cost-based electricity rates. This has the effect of increasing the demand for the higher-cost power. See, supra, fn. 18. The Federal Energy Regulatory Commission took over the determination of avoided cost in 1995.

[21] Wind technologies were practical for only very small numbers of residential and business consumers, and the same proved true for geothermal and ocean technologies.

[22] See fn. 10, supra. Under current law, wind facilities must be in service by the end of 2012 to qualify for the credit; for other eligible technologies the qualifying date is the end of 2013.

[23] Respectively, in the 2008 Energy Improvement and Extension Act (part of the Troubled Asset Relief Program), at http://thomas.loc.gov/cgi-bin/query/F?c110:1:./temp/~c110lPLkXb:e137069:; and "The American Recovery and Reinvestment Tax Act of 2009" (the stimulus bill), at http://thomas.loc.gov/home/h1/Recovery_Bill_Div_B.pdf. The 2009 legislation allows facilities that qualify for the production tax credit to choose instead to take either the federal business energy investment credit or an equivalent cash grant. The latter two subsidies generally are 30 percent of eligible costs. Note that the investment tax credit/cash grant is based upon the capital cost of the renewable generation capacity and thus is independent of the amount of electricity actually produced. See Browner, Klain, and Summers, op. cit., fn. 16 above. With a few exceptions, facilities are eligible for the production tax credit for ten years.

[24] Examples include renewable-energy grants from the Treasury Department, various grant and loan guarantee programs from the Agriculture Department, and loan guarantee programs from the Energy Department. Again, see the various summaries provided at http://www.dsireusa.org/.

At the state level, policies in support of renewable-energy investment and production vary widely; examples are production tax credits, property- and sales-tax exemptions, and subsidized loans. An important indirect subsidy results from standard regulatory ratemaking: Higher-cost power is combined (or *bundled*) with lower-cost power in regulated rates, which reflect average costs across different electricity-generation technologies and across peak and off-peak periods.[25] Even more important are the current legal/regulatory RPS requirements in many states for the use of renewable-energy sources for given percentages of the respective state's generation, consumption, or sales of electricity in the context of some timetable.[26] Table 1-1 shows the thirty states (plus the District of Columbia) with RPS requirements and the seven states with RPS goals not yet mandatory.

---

[25] For a more detailed discussion, see Robert L. Bradley Jr., "Renewable Energy: Not Cheap, Not '-Green,'" Cato Institute policy analysis no. 280, August 27, 1997, pp. 7–8, at http://www. cato.org/pub_display.php?pub_id=1139. See also supra, fn. 18 and fn. 20.

[26] For example, the California RPS, enacted in 2002 and accelerated in 2006 and 2007, mandated that electricity-supply corporations increase procurement from eligible renewable-energy resources by at least 1 percent of their retail sales annually until they reach 20 percent by 2010. See California Senate bill 1078, chapter 516, enacted September 12, 2002, at http://www.energy.ca.gov/portfolio/documents/documents/SB1078.PDF; California Senate bill 107, chapter 464, enacted September 26, 2006, at http://energyalmanac.ca.gov/renewables/rps/sb_107_bill_20060926_chaptered.pdf; and California Senate bill 1036, chapter 685, enacted October 14, 2007, at http://www.energy.ca.gov/renewables/documents/sb_1036_bill_20071014_chaptered.pdf. In addition, executive orders issued by Governor Arnold Schwarzenegger in 2008 and 2009 established a further RPS goal of 33 percent by 2020, directing the California Air Resources Board (CARB) to adopt regulations to achieve that end. See Executive Order S-14-08, November 17, 2008, at http://www.dmg.gov/documents/EO_S_14_08_Renewable_Energy_CA_111708.pdf; and Executive Order S-21-09, September 15, 2009, at http://www.pewclimate.org/docUploads/CA%20Exec%20order%20S-21-09.PDF. See also the California Public Utilities Commission (CPUC), "Renewables Portfolio Standard Quarterly Report, 3rd Quarter 2010," at http://www.cpuc.ca.gov/NR/rdonlyres/6472286E-6372-47CF-9F3D-2D2C3 100BF6D/0/Q32010QuarterlyRPSReporttotheLegislature.pdf. Figure 1, op. cit., p. 3, shows installed RPS capacity for California in 2010 at 1401 MW. Data from the California Energy Commission show 2009 RPS generation for the three large investor-owned utilities (Pacific Gas and Electric, San Diego Gas and Electric, and Southern California Edison) at 27.3 terawatt-hours (thousand gigawatt-hours), out of total deliveries of 217.4 tWh, or 12.6 percent. For 2010, the estimated figures are, respectively, 28.3 tWh, 217.9 tWh, and 13.0 percent (taken from private communication with CPUC staff and unpublished CPUC projections). To the extent that the California experience is representative, these numbers suggest that achievement of the RPS goals is not a trivial undertaking. On April 12, 2011, Governor Jerry Brown signed legislation elevating the 33 percent RPS standard into a legal requirement; see http://leginfo.ca.gov/pub/11-12/bill/sen/sb_0001-0050/sbx1_2_bill_20110412_chaptered.pdf.

TABLE 1-1

RENEWABLE PORTFOLIO STANDARDS

(PERCENT OF ELECTRICITY SALES EXCEPT WHERE NOTED)

State	Requirement/Goal*
Arizona	15 by 2025
California	33 by 2020
Colorado	20 by 2020
Connecticut	27 by 2020
Delaware	20 by 2019
District of Columbia	20 by 2020
Hawaii	20 by 2020
Illinois	25 by 2025
Iowa	105 MW by 2025
Kansas	20 by 2020
Maine	30 by 2000
Maryland	20 by 2022
Massachusetts	various requirements
Michigan	10 by 2015
Minnesota	25 by 2020
Missouri	15 by 2021
Montana	15 by 2015
Nevada	20 by 2015
New Hampshire	23.8 (16.3 new) by 2025
New Jersey	22.5 by 2021
New Mexico	10 or 20 by 2020
New York	24 by 2013
North Carolina	10/12.5 by 2018/2021
North Dakota	10 by 2015
Ohio	25 by 2025
Oklahoma	15 by 2015
Oregon	5–10 or 25 by 2025
Pennsylvania	18 by 5/31/2021

State	Requirement/Goal*
Rhode Island	16 by 2020
South Dakota	10 by 2015
Texas	5880 MW by 2015
Utah	20 by 2025
Vermont	20 by 2017
Virginia	12 of 2007 sales by 2022
Washington	15 by 2020
West Virginia	25 by 2025
Wisconsin	10 by 12/31/2015

SOURCE: U.S. Environmental Protection Agency, at http://www.epa.gov/chp/state-policy/renewable_
fs.html; and various pages, at http://www.dsireusa.org/incentives/. These two sources provide information on numerous restrictions, limitations, and qualifications imposed respectively by the states
with respect to different classes of power producers and different renewable technologies.
NOTE: *Figures for Oklahoma, North Dakota, South Dakota, Utah, Vermont, Virginia, and West Virginia (renewables) are nonmandatory goals.

It is useful to examine U.S. generating capacity for renewables—the
amount of power that renewable production facilities could produce in
theory at a given moment—and actual renewable production, in comparison with conventional sources and hydroelectric power. Table 1-2 presents
data on summer electric-generation capacity for conventional and renewable facilities for the United States in 2005 through 2009.[27]

Hydroelectric generating capacity is by far the largest component of
total renewable capacity but changed virtually not at all over the five-
year period even as total renewable capacity grew by about 27 GW, or
27.5 percent. Almost all of that increase was in wind capacity. Note also
from table 1-5, in this chapter's appendix, following, that every state
with an RPS requirement or goal includes wind generation or capacity as

---

[27] Data for electric generation are presented in table 1-3 below. Generation capacity and actual
generation are not strictly proportional because alternative generation technologies have different
capacity factors (the ratio of actual output over a time period to the output that would have been
observed had the facility been operated at full capacity for that time period) and are designed for use
in different ways, etc. See also the data summaries for the individual states on renewable-generation
capacity and net generation at http://www.eia.doe.gov/cneaf/solar.renewables/page/state_profiles/
r_profiles_sum.html?featureclicked=3&.

TABLE 1-2
U.S. GENERATING CAPACITY
(GIGAWATTS)

Source	2005	2006	2007	2008	2009
Biomass	9.8	10.1	10.8	11.1	11.4
Waste	3.6	3.7	4.1	4.2	4.4
Landfill gas	0.9	1.0	1.3	1.4	1.5
MSW	2.2	2.2	2.2	2.2	2.2
Other	0.6	0.6	0.6	0.6	0.7
Wood	6.2	6.4	6.7	6.9	6.9
Geothermal	2.3	2.3	2.2	2.3	2.4
Solar thermal/PV	0.4	0.4	0.5	0.5	0.6
Wind	8.7	11.3	16.5	24.7	33.5
Non-hydro renewable	21.2	24.1	30.1	38.5	47.8
Hydroelectric	77.5	77.8	77.9	77.9	78.0
Total renewable	98.7	101.9	108.0	116.4	125.8
Total nonrenewable	879.3	884.3	886.9	893.7	901.8
Total	978.0	986.2	994.9	1,010.2	1,027.6
Non-hydro renewable/total (%)	2.2	2.4	3.0	3.8	4.7

SOURCE: U.S. Energy Information Administration, at http://www.eia.gov/cneaf/solar.renewables/page/table4.html.
NOTES: MSW—municipal solid waste; PV—photovoltaics. Columns may not sum due to rounding and/or categories not shown. Hydroelectric excludes pumped storage. A gigawatt equals one billion watts.

a qualifying source, and the same is true for almost every state with respect to solar-thermal generation and/or solar-photovoltaic technology as qualifying sources.

Table 1-3 presents recent data on actual electric generation from renewables; the data show the same general patterns as those for generation capacity in table 1-2.

From tables 1-2 and 1-3 we see that electric generation from non-hydroelectric renewable sources as a proportion of total generation has

TABLE 1-3
U.S. ELECTRICITY GENERATION
(TERAWATT-HOURS)

Source	2005	2006	2007	2008	2009
Biomass	54.3	54.9	55.5	55.0	54.3
Waste	15.4	16.1	16.5	17.7	18.1
Landfill gas	5.1	5.7	6.2	7.2	7.4
MSW	8.3	8.5	8.3	8.1	8.3
Other	1.9	1.9	2.1	2.5	2.4
Wood	38.9	38.8	39.0	37.3	36.2
Geothermal	14.7	14.6	14.6	15.0	15.2
Solar thermal/PV	0.6	0.5	0.6	0.9	0.8
Wind	17.8	26.6	34.4	55.4	70.8
Non-hydro renewable	87.3	96.5	105.2	26.2	141.1
Hydroelectric	270.3	289.2	247.5	254.8	272.1
Total renewable	357.7	385.8	352.7	381.0	413.2
Total nonrenewable	3,697.7	3,678.9	3,804.0	3,738.4	3,539.9
Total	4,055.4	4,064.7	4,156.7	4,119.4	3,953.1
Non-hydro renewable/total (%)	2.2	2.4	2.5	3.1	3.6

SOURCES: U.S. Energy Information Administration, at http://www.eia.gov/cneaf/solar.renewables/page/
table3.html and http://www.eia.doe.gov/cneaf/electricity/epm/table1_1.html.
NOTES: See table 1-2. A terawatt-hour equals one trillion watt-hours.

tended to be a bit below its proportional share of total generation capacity. This outcome is the result of the lower availability (capacity factor) characterizing renewable power technologies relative to conventional generation capacity; if renewable capacity grows as a proportion of total capacity, this problem is likely to increase in importance, as discussed in more detail in chapter 2. As noted above,[28] the California RPS mandate for 2010 was 20 percent, but the actual figure for 2010 was about 13

---

[28] See fn. 26.

TABLE 1-4
NON-HYDROELECTRIC RENEWABLE GENERATION, 2008
(PERCENT OF TOTAL GENERATION)

State	Percent
Arizona	0.1
California	11.9
Colorado	6.1
Connecticut	2.4
Delaware	2.2
District of Columbia	n/a
Hawaii	6.8
Illinois	1.5
Iowa	8.0
Kansas	3.8
Maine	2.4
Maryland	1.3
Massachusetts	3.0
Michigan	2.3
Minnesota	10.7
Missouri	0.3
Montana	2.8
Nevada	4.4
New Hampshire	5.1
New Jersey	1.4
New Mexico	4.5
New York	2.4
North Carolina	1.5
North Dakota	5.2
Ohio	0.4
Oklahoma	3.3
Oregon	9.8

State	Percent
Pennsylvania	1.3
Rhode Island	2.1
South Dakota	2.1
Texas	4.4
Utah	0.6
Vermont	6.2
Virginia	3.7
Washington	4.5
West Virginia	0.4
Wisconsin	2.8
United States (all states)	*3.1*

SOURCE: EIA, at http://www.eia.doe.gov/cneaf/solar.renewables/page/state_profiles/r_profiles_sum.html?featureclicked=3&, and author computations.
NOTE: n/a—not applicable.

percent for the three large investor-owned utilities. Table 1-4 presents data for 2008 on non-hydroelectric renewable generation as a proportion of total generation for the thirty-seven states listed in table 1-1.

As a crude generalization, these market shares are small, particularly given the policies and mandates imposed to support and hasten the adoption of renewable generation technologies in these states.[29] This suggests that there may exist some fundamental problems (or barriers) that afflict renewable technologies disproportionately, a topic to which we turn in chapter 2.

---

[29] Michaels, op. cit., fn. 13 above, pp. 14–16, has a useful discussion of the problems encountered by several states pursuing achievement of their RPS mandates.

Appendix to Chapter 1

Table 1-5 shows the alternative- and renewable-energy sources and technologies that may be counted toward the respective RPS requirements and goals summarized in table 1-1.

TABLE 1-5

ELIGIBLE RPS TECHNOLOGIES

State	A	B	C	D	E	F	G	H	I	J	K	L	M	N	O	P
Arizona	•	•	•			•	•	•			•	•				•
California	•	•				•	•	•	•	•	•	•	•		•	•
Colorado	•	•	•			•	•	•			•					•
Connecticut	•	•	•	•	•		•	•	•	•	•	•	•		•	•
Delaware	•	•				•	•	•		•	•	•	•		•	•
D. of Columbia	•	•				•	•	•	•	•	•	•	•		•	•
Hawaii	•	•	•	•		•	•	•	•	•	•	•	•		•	•
Illinois	•	•		•			•	•			•	•				•
Iowa	•	•					•	•	•							•
Kansas	•	•					•	•	•		•	•				•
Maine	•	•			•	•	•	•			•	•	•		•	•
Maryland	•	•				•	•	•	•	•	•	•	•		•	•
Massachusetts	•	•	•			•	•	•	•	•	•	•	•		•	•
Michigan	•	•	•	•		•	•	•	•		•	•	•		•	•
Minnesota	•	•			•		•	•	•		•	•				•
Missouri	•	•				•	•	•	•		•	•				•

State	A	B	C	D	E	F	G	H	I	J	K	L	M	N	O	P
Montana	•	•				•	•	•			•	•				•
Nevada	•	•	•	•		•	•	•	•		•	•		•		•
New Hampshire	•	•			•	•	•	•	•	•	•	•	•		•	•
New Jersey	•	•			•	•	•	•	•		•	•	•			•
New Mexico	•	•				•	•	•			•	•				•
New York	•	•			•		•	•		•	•		•			•
North Carolina	•	•	•	•		•	•	•			•	•	•		•	•
North Dakota	•	•	•			•	•	•			•	•				•
Ohio	•	•	•	•	•	•	•	•	•	•	•	•	•		•	•
Oklahoma	•	•		•		•	•	•	•		•	•				•
Oregon	•	•			•	•	•	•		•	•	•	•	•		•
Pennsylvania	•	•	•	•	•	•	•	•	•		•	•				•
Rhode Island	•	•				•	•	•		•	•		•	•	•	•
South Dakota	•	•	•			•	•	•	•		•	•	•		•	•
Texas	•	•				•	•	•		•	•	•	•		•	•
Utah	•	•	•			•	•	•		•	•	•	•		•	•
Vermont	•	•				•	•	•			•	•				•
Virginia	•	•				•	•	•		•	•	•	•		•	•
Washington	•	•	•	•		•	•	•		•	•	•	•			•
West Virginia	•	•			•	•	•	•	•		•	•				•
Wisconsin	•	•				•	•	•			•	•	•		•	•

SOURCE: U.S. Environmental Protection Agency, at http://www.epa.gov/chp/state-policy/renewable_fs.html; and various pages, at http://www.dsireusa.org/incentives/.
NOTES: A-biofuels; B-biomass; C-combined heat and power (renewable), waste heat; D-efficiency; E-fuel cells (nonrenewable); F-geothermal; G-hydro; H-landfill gas; I-municipal waste; J-ocean thermal; K-photovoltaic; L-solar thermal; M-tidal; N-waste tire; O-wave; P-wind.

2

Problems Afflicting
Renewable Energy
in Electricity Generation

The combination of substantial policy support for expanded use of renewable-energy sources for electricity generation and small market shares—as well as the observed shift in many states toward mandated RPS requirements—suggests that important constraints inherent in renewable technology have impeded the adoption of renewable-electricity generation.[30] Indeed, a reading of the technical literature reveals several themes that seem not to have received widespread attention in the popular discussion. These intrinsic problems can be denoted as

- the unconcentrated energy content of renewable-energy sources

- location (or siting) limitations

- relatively low availability (*capacity factors*) over time combined with the intermittent nature of wind flows and sunlight.[31]

---

[30] The adoption of RPS mandates, on the other hand, may represent simple manifestations of the politics of wealth redistribution—rent seeking by interest groups—rather than technological (or cost) problems. See also fn. 18, supra. However, the continuing and prospective market-share difficulties experienced by renewable technologies nonetheless suggest strongly the importance of technological difficulties. The two hypotheses are not mutually exclusive.

[31] The capacity factor for a generation facility (or technology) is its actual production over a given time period divided by its theoretical maximum production over that time period. See fn. 27, supra.

19

Unconcentrated Energy Content

The energy content of wind flows and sunlight depends on air speed and sunlight intensity, in contrast with the concentrated nature of the energy contained in fossil or nuclear fuels.[32] In order to compensate for this unconcentrated nature of renewable-energy sources, large capital investments in land and/or materials must be made to make renewable generation even technically practical in terms of generating nontrivial amounts of electricity. A wind farm would require five hundred windmills of 2 MW each to provide a theoretical generation capacity of 1,000 MW.[33] Since the wind turbines must be spaced apart to avoid wake effects,[34] a 1,000 MW wind farm might require on the order of forty-eight thousand to sixty-four thousand acres (or seventy-five to one hundred square miles) of land.[35] With an assumed capacity factor for a typical wind farm of, say, 35 percent,[36]

---

[32] See Vaclav Smil, *Energy at the Crossroads: Global Perspectives and Uncertainties*, Cambridge: MIT Press, 2003, pp. 276–278. Energy concentration in simple terms is the energy content of a given fuel per volume. Huber and Mills note that coal supplies about twice as much energy as wood on a pound-for-pound basis, while oil provides about twice as much as coal, and a gram of uranium 235 has as much energy as four tons of coal: "Historically, we have always pursued fuels that pack more energy in less space." See Peter W. Huber and Mark P. Mills, *The Bottomless Well: The Twilight of Fuel, the Virtue of Waste, and Why We Will Never Run Out of Energy*, New York: Basic Books, 2005, p. 8.

[33] Note that the average nameplate capacities of wind turbines installed in the United States in 2007, 2008, and 2009 were, respectively, 1.65 MW, 1.66 MW, and 1.74 MW. See the U.S. Department of Energy, "2009 Wind Technologies Market Report," August 2010, p. v, at http://www1.eere.energy.gov/windandhydro/pdfs/2009_wind_technologies_market_report.pdf.

[34] *Wake effects* are interferences with wind speeds for a given turbine caused by other turbines in a wind farm. The usual assumed spacing requirement is five to ten turbine diameters apart. See http://www.nrel.gov/analysis/power_databook/calc_wind.php. Smil, op. cit., fn. 32 above, p. 276, discusses turbine-spacing requirements and theoretical limits on the amount of energy that can be extracted from wind flows. He notes that a generalized computation of the energy content of wind flows in terms of a watts-per-square-meter metric would require "a number of nested assumptions." Nonetheless, there is little dissent in the literature from the proposition that the energy content of wind flows is highly diffuse. Note that the energy content of wind increases with the cube of the change in wind speed, so that a doubling of the latter increases the former by a factor of eight. Crudely, wind turbines begin to produce power when wind speeds reach about 5 mph, reach rated capacity at about 30–35 mph, and are designed to shut down at about 50–55 mph in order to prevent damage from storms.

[35] For a further discussion, see Bradley, supra, fn. 25, p. 11.

[36] See Vaclav Smil, *Energy Myths and Realities: Bringing Science to the Energy Policy Debate* (Washington, D.C.: AEI Press, 2010), 123–125. A capacity factor of 36 percent was assumed by John P. Harper et al., "Wind Project Financing Structures: A Review and Comparative Analysis," Ernest Orlando Lawrence Berkeley National Laboratory, LBNL-63434, September 2007, p. 61, table B1, at http://eetd.lbl.gov/EA/EMP/reports/63434.pdf. That is the highest currently assumed capacity factor for on-shore wind power that I have seen in the literature. See also fn. 42 below.

reliable wind capacity of 1,000 MW would require an amount of land (perhaps at different locations) on the order of three times that rough estimate.[37] In contrast, a 1,000 MW gas-fired plant requires about ten to fifteen acres; conventional coal, natural gas, and nuclear plants have capacity factors of 85 to 90 percent.

An analogous problem characterizes solar power. The energy content of sunlight, crudely, is about 150 to 400 watts per square meter, depending on location, of which about 20 to 30 percent is convertible to electricity, depending on the particular technology.[38] Accordingly, even in theory a square meter of solar energy receiving capacity is enough to power roughly one 100-watt light bulb, putting aside such capacity-factor issues as sunlight intensity and the like. This problem of land requirements for solar-thermal facilities is of sufficient importance that most analyses assume a maximum capacity of 50 to 100 MW, which, conservatively, would require approximately 1,250 acres, or two square miles.

In short, transformation of the unconcentrated energy content of wind and sunlight into a form usable for modern applications requires massive capital investment in the form of both land and wind turbines and solar-receiving equipment. The diffusion problem means that the energy that can be extracted from renewable sources, relative to that from conventional forms, is limited by its very nature. Smil notes that the "mismatch between the low power densities of renewable energy flows and relatively high power densities of modern final energy uses means that any large-scale diffusion of [renewable] energy conversions will require a profound spatial restructuring, engendering major environmental and socioeconomic impacts."[39]

---

[37] Some of the land used by wind farms but not actually bearing turbines, other equipment, or access roads might remain available for farming or other purposes. Such considerations are highly site specific, and no systematic data on this issue seem to be available. For a skeptical discussion, see Robert Bryce, *Power Hungry* (New York: Public Affairs, 2010), 84–85.

[38] See Smil, supra, fn. 32, pp. 240 and 284–285.

[39] Smil, supra, fn. 32, p. 243.

Siting Limitations and Transmission Costs

Conventional power-generation plants can be sited, in principle, almost anywhere, and such fuels as coal and natural gas can be transported to the generation facilities. This means that investment-planning decisions can optimize transmission-investment costs along with the other numerous factors that constrain and shape generation-investment choices, among them reliability issues, transmission-line losses, and the like. Wind and solar sites, on the other hand, must be placed where the wind blows and the sun shines with sufficient intensity and duration.[40] Because appropriate sites are limited, with the most useful (that is, lowest cost) ones exploited first, the marginal cost of exploiting such sites must rise, so that even if wind and solar technologies exhibit important scale economies in terms of capacity and/or generation costs, scale economies may not characterize a broader cost calculation including the cost of finding and using particular sites.[41] In other words, scale economies may not be present at the industry level even if they are present at the project (or even the turbine or parabolic dish) level. This reality is consistent with a time series of capacity factors for 1998–2009 published recently by the Energy Information Administration. The capacity factors for non-hydroelectric renewables declined almost monotonically from 57 percent to 33.9 percent, suggesting that as renewables capacity has expanded it has been forced onto increasingly unfavorable sites.[42]

Because conventional-generation investments can optimize transmission costs and reliability factors more easily than is the case for wind and solar capacity, it would be surprising if such costs were not higher for the

---

[40] Photovoltaic installations, far more suitable for small applications, face this problem to a lesser degree relative to solar-thermal installations, as a crude generalization, but still are constrained by the availability and intensity of sunlight.

[41] Smil, supra, fn. 32, pp. 275–278, discusses some engineering realities that may cast doubt on an assumption of scale economies even at the project level. The available data on scale economies are discussed here in chapter 4.

[42] See U.S. Energy Information Administration, *Electric Power Annual 2009*, revised April 2011, at http://www.eia.gov/cneaf/electricity/epa/epat5p2.html. Between 1998 and 2009, non-hydro-renewables capacity increased from 16.3 GW to 47.8 GW. See EIA, at http://www.eia.doe.gov/cneaf/solar. renewables/page/table4.html.

latter.[43] This general condition is exacerbated by the physical realities that conditions for wind generation are strongest in open plains regions, while solar generation in general requires regions with strong sunlight and, for solar-thermal plants, sizable open areas. For the United States, the best wind-capacity sites are in a region stretching from the Northern Plains down through Texas, and the best solar-thermal sites are in the Southwest. The United States simply lacks significant east-west high-voltage inter-connection transmission capacity to transport such power to the coasts.[44] One national study of this problem notes that "wind development will require substantial additions to the nation's transmission infrastructure... due to the locational dependence of wind resources [and] the relatively low capacity factor of wind plants."[45]

Some analyses of these transmission costs are available.[46] Mills et al., in a survey of forty transmission studies conducted from 2001 to 2008,

---

[43] Note that in a strict economic sense the meaning of *lower* or *higher* cost is a bit problematic, in that the relative market values of sites with lower and higher costs should reflect those respective differences so that the economic costs of using alternative sites should be equal (in "equilibrium"). This somewhat esoteric point will be ignored here, but it suggests that neither scale economies nor scale diseconomies would be present at the industry level. Once the cost benefits of learning—downward shifts in cost rather than a movement along a declining portion of an average cost function—were attained, no further economies in terms of the average cost of using a given renewable technology would be available. Again, strictly speaking, even "learning" might not reduce true economic costs fully because the labor or capital embodying such knowledge ought to command a higher (factor) price reflecting the market value of that knowledge.

[44] See Smil, supra, fn. 32, pp. 298–299. In a recent decision, the U.S. Court of Appeals for the Ninth Circuit ruled that the U.S. Department of Energy had failed to follow proper administrative procedures when it established national interest corridors for new high-voltage transmission lines in ten states. The plaintiffs were a coalition of environmental groups, notwithstanding their strong adver-tised support for RPS standards and the expansion of renewable-electricity generation. See *California Wilderness Coalition v. U.S. Department of Energy*, case 08-71074, published February 1, 2011, at http://www.ca9.uscourts.gov/datastore/opinions/2011/02/01/08-71074.pdf.

[45] See Andrew Mills, Ryan Wiser, and Kevin Porter, "The Cost of Transmission for Wind Energy: A Review of Transmission Planning Studies," Ernest Orlando Lawrence Berkeley National Laboratory, LBNL-1471E, February 2009, p. vii, at http://eetd.lbl.gov/EA/EMP/reports/lbnl-1471e.pdf.

[46] The Federal Energy Regulatory Commission (FERC), in a recent case involving the Midwest Independent Transmission System Operator, ruled that the transmission costs attributable to wind generation may be allocated to consumers regardless of the amount of wind power actually consumed by any given ratepayer. This ruling essentially spreads such costs across the entire grid; accordingly, the transmission costs associated with wind generation are not reduced but instead are hidden some-what from calculations of the marginal cost of wind power. See the FERC Conditional Order, Docket No. ER10-1791-000, December 16, 2010, at http://www.ferc.gov/whats-new/comm-meet/2010/121610/E-1.pdf.

find a median transmission cost of $15 per megawatt hour (mWh).[47] The survey was limited to studies of transmission requirements for multiple new wind plants with a combined capacity greater than 300 MW. As shown in table 2-1 below, conventional generation has transmission costs less than half those of wind generation and about a third those of solar thermal generation. An analysis by the California Public Utilities Commission (CPUC) concludes that implementation of a 20 percent RPS requirement for the state by 2020 would require four new major transmission lines at a cost of about $4 billion, while a 33 percent RPS standard would require seven new lines at a cost of $12 billion. Calculations provided in the CPUC report suggest that the analysis is problematic.[48]

A study done for the National Renewable Energy Laboratory examined the transmission requirements and attendant costs for four alternative wind-capacity scenarios for the Eastern Interconnection (the continental United States east of the Rocky Mountains, minus Texas, plus parts of southeastern Canada).[49] This study reports a cost of wind "integration" of

---

[47] Mills et al., supra, fn. 45, pp. 6–8. The cost figures are reported in nominal dollars (that is, unadjusted for inflation).

[48] See California Public Utilities Commission, "33% Renewables Portfolio Standard: Implementation Analysis Preliminary Results," June 2009, p. 1 and table 5, at http://www.cpuc.ca.gov/NR/rdonlyres/1865C207-FEB5-43CF-99EB-A212B78467F6/0/33PercentRPSImplementationAnalysisInterim Report.pdf. The CPUC projections imply about 310 million mWh of total California electricity consumption in 2020; current consumption is about 265 million mWh. That future consumption level in the CPUC analysis is virtually unaffected by price (or average cost), an outcome that calls the overall analysis into question. Another projection in the study that raises concerns is the conclusion that an all-gas power-production scenario in 2020 yields an average price only slightly lower than a 20 percent RPS reference case ($0.154 per kWh versus $0.158 per kWh); and the average price in the 33 percent reference case is only $0.011 higher, at $0.169 per kWh. Those differentials are not plausible unless they exclude important costs or subsidy considerations. In any event, if we assume 33 percent of that total consumption in 2020 is from renewables, a fifty-year life for the associated transmission lines, and a 5 percent real rate of interest, we have 102.3 million mWh of renewable power imposing an annual transmission cost of about $654 million, ignoring line losses, maintenance costs, and other factors. That works out to about $6.39 per mWh for transmission costs. Note that it is not clear whether the 20 percent or 33 percent RPS standard applies to capacity, generation, contracted power, or some other parameter. Michaels, supra, fn. 13, p. 12, has a useful discussion of the ways in which RPS compliance has been defined downward as achievement of the RPS mandates has proven elusive. Note also that because of the recent economic downturn and projected economic conditions in California, the transmission requirements and costs for 2020 assumed by the CPUC may be higher than would be the case were the analysis to be updated. See http://docs.cpuc.ca.gov/efile/RULC/127544.pdf and http://www.cpuc.ca.gov/PUC/energy/procurement/LTPP/ltpp_history.htm.

[49] See EnerNex Corporation, "Eastern Wind Integration and Transmission Study," NREL/SR-550-47086, January 2010, at http://www.nrel.gov/wind/systemsintegration/pdfs/2010/ewits_executive_summary.pdf, at tables 1–4 and figure 3.

about $5 per mWh, but the figures in the study suggest transmission costs higher than that figure. For wind generation at 20 percent of total generation, the study assumes a need for about 225,000 MW of wind-generation capacity, with total transmission costs of approximately $80 billion. If we assume a 30 percent capacity factor, we have wind generation for 2,628 hours per year. Assuming a fifty-year life for the transmission lines and a real interest rate of 5 percent, and ignoring line losses, maintenance costs, and other complexities, we have annual transmission costs of $4.4 billion spread across 591.3 million mWh. This works out to about $7.37 per mWh, a figure somewhat higher than the $5 per mWh integration calculation and double the transmission figures shown in table 2-1 (following) for conventional coal and natural gas generation. Figure 3 in the study suggests annual transmission costs of approximately $10 to 17 billion; if we use the $10 billion figure, transmission costs would be almost $17 per mWh, a figure roughly comparable to the $15 median reported in the Mills et al. survey noted above.[50]

A comprehensive comparison of various cost categories across generation types has been published by the Energy Information Administration as part of the 2010 *Annual Energy Outlook*.[51] Table 2-1 presents some of those projections for generation plants entering service in 2016.

The transmission figures for wind and solar generation are lower than those reported in the Mills et al. survey but are substantially higher than those projected for coal- or combined-cycle gas generation and are roughly comparable to the transmission cost projections for gas turbines.[52] These projections for transmission costs are consistent with the hypothesis that wind and solar power are highly constrained in terms of capacity factors and sites and so impose higher marginal dispatch and transmission costs than is the case for conventional generation.

---

[50] Ibid., p. 14.

[51] U.S. Energy Information Administration, "2016 Levelized Cost of New Generation Resources from the *Annual Energy Outlook 2010*," at http://www.eia.doe.gov/oiaf/aeo/pdf/2016levelized_costs_aeo2010.pdf.

[52] Note that the gas turbines have far lower capacity factors than is the case for coal or natural gas combined cycle generation because turbine variable costs are so much higher. Unlike most renewables, turbines are dispatchable but are likely to be called upon only during peak demands or when outages require the use of capacity with high operating costs. As a rough generalization, gas turbines are about 30 percent more costly to operate than combined-cycle gas units.

TABLE 2-1
EIA LEVELIZED COST PROJECTIONS, 2016
(2008 DOLLARS PER MWH)

Plant Type	Capacity Factor (%)	Levelized cost				
		Capital	Fixed O&M	Var. O&M	Trans-mission	Total
Natural gas						
adv. com. cycle	87	22.4	1.6	51.7	3.6	79.3
combined cycle	87	22.9	1.7	54.9	3.6	83.1
Conventional coal	85	69.2	3.8	23.9	3.6	100.4
Advanced coal	85	81.2	5.3	20.4	3.6	110.5
Biomass	83	73.3	9.1	24.9	3.8	111.0
Geothermal	90	88.0	22.9	0.0	4.8	115.7
Advanced nuclear	90	94.9	11.7	9.4	3.0	119.0
Hydroelectric	51.4	103.7	3.5	7.1	5.7	119.9
Natural gas adv. turbine	30	38.5	4.1	70.0	10.8	123.5
Natural gas conv. turbine	30	41.1	4.7	82.9	10.8	139.5
Wind (onshore)	34.4	130.5	10.4	0.0	8.4	149.3
Wind (offshore)	39.3	159.9	23.8	0.0	7.4	191.1
Solar thermal	31.2	224.4	21.8	0.0	10.4	256.6
Solar PV	21.7	376.8	6.4	0.0	13.0	396.1

SOURCE: See fn. 51.
NOTES: Levelized costs—per mWh, the sum of fixed and variable costs over the lifetime of a generating unit, averaged over the sum of total generation for that lifetime.
O&M—operations and maintenance.

Low Availability and Intermittency

Electric energy in large amounts cannot be stored at low cost in batteries due to technological limitations; only indirect storage in the form of water in dams is economical. This reality means that the production and consumption of electricity in a given power network must be balanced constantly in order to prevent blackouts and more generally to preserve system reliability. Because unexpected surges in demand and/or outages of generating equipment can occur, backup-generation capacity must be maintained; such backup capacity is termed the *operating reserve* for the given network. This operating reserve is of two types: The first is the *spinning reserve*, that is, generators already connected to the network, the output of which can be increased by raising the torque applied to the generating turbines. The typical system requirement is that spinning reserves be 50 percent or more of total operating reserves. The second component of operating reserves is the *supplemental reserve*, which comprises generation capacity that can be brought on line within five to ten minutes and/or electric power that can be obtained quickly from other networks or by withholding power being distributed to other networks. Additional reserve capacity often is provided by generators that require up to an hour to come on line; this backup capacity is not included in measures of the operating reserve for a system because of the length of time required for availability.

Electric-supply systems respond to growing demands (*load*) over the course of a day (or year) by increasing output from the lowest-cost generating units first and then calling upon successively more-expensive units as electric loads grow toward the daily (or seasonal) peak. As noted above, most electric-generation capacity fueled by renewable energy sources is not dispatchable—that is, it is not available on demand. In other words, system planning and optimization cannot be based on an assumption that it will be available to provide power to the grid when it is expected to be most economical. Accordingly, it cannot be scheduled: it requires backup generation capacity to preserve system reliability.[53] Because wind and solar generation is intermittent, depending on wind and sunlight conditions, a recent study of the operational impacts of increasing RPS mandates for the California electricity system noted that "the variability and high-ramping characteristics of renewable generation create operational issues."[54] Without backup generation and/or power

[53] See, e.g., EIA, "Impacts of a 15-Percent Renewable Portfolio Standard," report no. SR-OIAF/2007-03, June 2007, at http://www.eia.doe.gov/oiaf/servicerpt/prps/rps.html.
[54] KEMA, Inc., "Research Evaluation of Wind Generation, Solar Generation, and Storage Impact on the California Grid," June 2010, p. 1, at http://www.ovcr.ucla.edu/uploads/file/CA%20Energy%20 Commission_PIER%20Final%20Project%20Report_June%202010.pdf.

storage,[55] one conclusion in that study is that "system performance degraded, in terms of maximum area control error excursions and North American Electric Reliability Corporation control performance standards, significantly for 20 percent renewables penetration and became extreme [sic] at 33 percent renewables penetration, using the same automatic generation control strategies and amounts of regulation services as today."[56]

The study, using figures from the California Independent System Operator, projects that the increase in renewable generation capacity between 2009 and 2020 would be about 17.7 GW for the 20 percent RPS standard and about 22.4 GW in the 33 percent case.[57] The projected needs for backup capacity (of varying types) are, respectively, 0.8 GW and 4.8 GW, in the absence of battery storage.[58] For the 20 percent RPS standard, that backup requirement is 4.5 percent (0.8/17.7); for the 33 percent RPS standard, the projection (21 percent) is about the same as that reported in Kreutzer et al. (citing a National Renewable Energy Laboratory [NREL] study) of a need for 0.2 MW of backup capacity for each MW of wind capacity.[59]

Several studies have concluded that wind capacity does not impose large costs on a given power system as long as the wind generation remains about 10 percent or less of system output, because the intermittent nature of wind resources to a degree has effects similar to those of unexpected outages and other familiar problems afflicting conventional

---

[55] That study argues that current battery technology is sufficient to manage the integration of renewables in an electric power grid. See ibid., pp. 3–4 and 65.

[56] Ibid., pp. 2–3.

[57] This includes photovoltaic, solar-thermal, and wind generation. The 2009 figure cited is 3.8 GW, and the low/high average for 2020 is about 20.1 GW. See ibid., p. 28, table 3.

[58] See ibid., pp. 3–4.

[59] See David W. Kreutzer et al., "A Renewable Electricity Standard: What It Will Really Cost Americans," Heritage Foundation Center for Data Analysis, report no. 10-03, May 5, 2010, at http://heritage.org/Research/Reports/2010/05/A-Renewable-Electricity-Standard-What-It-Will-Really-Cost-Americans.

[60] For a discussion, see Smil, supra, fn. 36, pp. 125–128. Michaels, supra, fn. 13, p. 21, makes a similar point. Note that this does not mean that wind generation necessarily is economic at 10 percent or less of total system generation; it means only that the wind generation tends not to impose higher system costs due to intermittency. It still may be higher in cost for other reasons; and, as discussed below, the power produced by wind capacity is likely to be worth less than power produced by dispatchable units because of the inverse correlation between wind strength and peak demands, both daily and seasonal.

generation.[60] At the same time, outages of wind capacity due to weak wind conditions are much more likely to be correlated geographically than outages of conventional plants for the obvious reason that weak winds in part of a given region are likely to be observed in tandem with weak winds in other parts of that region. Because appropriate regions for solar-thermal sites and photovoltaic systems are concentrated geographically, the same correlation problem is likely to affect solar-electric generation as well.

In short, expansion of renewable power generation requires ancillary investment in backup capacity using conventional (dispatchable) technologies. From table 1-2 above we see that wind and solar renewables generation capacity in 2009 was about 34,000 MW. If we assume, conservatively, that this intermittent capacity has required investment in backup capacity of about 3 percent (rather than 4.5 percent), that latter investment would be about 1,000 MW. If we assume further an equal mix of coal-fired and combined-cycle gas-fired backup generation and, again conservatively, a capacity factor of 50 percent for the backup generators, cost estimates from the EIA suggest that this backup capacity has imposed fixed capital and operation and maintenance (O&M) costs of about $1.7 billion, variable operating costs of approximately $2 to $4.50 per mWh, and total costs per mWh of about $368.[61]

That rough estimate may be biased downward. Because state RPS mandates either implicitly or explicitly require system operators to take renewable power when it is available, conventional generation must be cycled—that is, in effect turned on and off—in coordination with the availability of the renewable generation. In particular for coal-fired generation, but also for gas combined-cycle backup generation, this means that the conventional assets cannot be operated as efficiently as would be the case were they not cycled up and down in response to wind- or solar-generation conditions. Note that gas turbines are significantly

---

[61] Author computations. See EIA, "Electricity Market Module," April 2010, p. 91, table 8.2, at http://www.eia.gov/oiaf/aeo/assumption/pdf/electricity.pdf#page=3. These numbers differ from those presented in table 2-1 above because they are not levelized. However, these EIA estimates are an effort to compare real resource costs across technologies—that is, without consideration of the effects of subsidies.

more expensive to operate than combined-cycle gas units, but the former are designed to respond to fluctuations in load conditions, and so their use as backup for renewables may not be inefficient despite the higher costs. In a study of the attendant emissions effects for Colorado and Texas, Bentek Energy concludes that RPS standards for the use of wind power impose significant operating and capital costs because of cycling needs for backup generation—particularly coal plants—and actually exacerbate air-pollution problems.[62] A more general technical analysis of this phenomenon has been developed by Hawkins.[63]

From table 2-1 above, we see that the EIA projects wind (onshore) and solar costs in 2016 at about $149 and $257 to $396 (all 2008 dollars) per mWh, respectively; these costs are substantially higher than those for gas- or coal-fired generation, at about $80 to $110 per mWh. These estimates are roughly consistent with the findings in a new paper by Tra, which finds that a 1 percentage point increase in an RPS requirement yields increases in commercial and residential electric utility rates between 4 and 10 percent.[64]

The higher cost of electricity generated with renewable-energy sources is only one side of the competitiveness question; the other is the value of that generation, as not all electricity is created equal. In particular, power generation, whether during a given daily cycle or across annual seasons. In this context, wind generation in particular is problematic, because in general there is an inverse relationship between the daily hours of peak demand and wind velocities and between peak summertime demands and peak wintertime wind velocities: winds tend to blow at night and in the winter.[65]

---

[62] See Bentek Energy, LLC, "How Less Became More: Wind, Power and Unintended Consequences in the Colorado Energy Market," April 16, 2010, pp. 25–33, at http://www.wind-watch.org/documents/wp-content/uploads/BENTEK-How-Less-Became-More.pdf.

[63] See Kent Hawkins, parts I–V, part I beginning at http://www.masterresource.org/2009/11/wind-integration-incremental-emissions-from-back-up-generation-cycling-part-i-a-framework-and-calculator/.

[64] Constant I. Tra, "Have Renewable Portfolio Standards Raised Electricity Rates? Evidence from U.S. Electric Utilities," unpublished manuscript, July 7, 2010, available from the author upon request.

[65] See also fn. 34, supra.

In a new paper, Joskow argues that standard comparisons of levelized costs have the effect of overvaluing such intermittent generating technologies as wind power relative to conventional generation that is dispatchable.[66] Generating units that cannot supply reliable power when it is most valuable have economic values lower than alternatives that can; but our system of subsidizing renewable sources of electricity both higher in cost and lower in value in effect is based on the opposite assumption.[67] This is a problem that is important for wind generation in particular because the output of wind facilities is disproportionately off-peak. Solar generation tends to have the opposite characteristic: it is strongest during periods of peak daytime demand and during the summer. Joskow notes that relative to wind, "solar-thermal plants have much more attractive production profiles...[and] similarly for photovoltaic technology output....So, solar technology may have a higher levelized cost than wind technology, but it may produce much more valuable electricity. Levelized cost calculations hide this important factor."[68]

Despite these important problems, no state has abandoned or weakened its RPS requirements, at least formally, and federal policies to promote renewable technology in electricity production remain in place. A number of arguments in support of these state and federal policies continue to enjoy substantial currency and support, a critique of which is the focus of chapter 3.

---

[66] See Paul L. Joskow, "Comparing the Costs of Intermittent and Dispatchable Electricity Generating Technologies," September 27, 2010, at http://econ-www.mit.edu/files/5989.

[67] Joskow notes that this problem is not relevant for comparisons of dispatchable generation technologies (e.g., coal versus natural gas) because the values of the electricity produced by dispatchable units are more or less the same. See ibid., pp. 2–4 and 9–12.

[68] Ibid., p. 21.

3

Central Rationales for Policy Support for Renewables: A Review

The arguments that have been marshaled in favor of public policy support for expansion of renewable power production are numerous and varied but generally fall into the following categories:

- renewable energy as an *infant industry*,

- leveling the playing field: offsets for the subsidies enjoyed by conventional generation,

- the adverse environmental effects of conventional generation,

- resource depletion or *sustainability*, and

- renewable electricity as a source of expanded green employment.

The Infant-Industry Argument

This rationale essentially assumes that new technologies often cannot compete with established ones because the available market at the beginning is too small for important scale economies to be exploited and because the downward shifts in costs that might result from a learning process, again, cannot be achieved without a substantial expansion in market share.[69]

---

[69] See fn. 43, supra. The presence of scale economies means operation along a downward sloping portion of the average cost function so that expanded output reduces average cost. Such economies of scale are not a necessary feature of any given production process, although they are likely to be present over some range of output in capital-intensive industries. Learning economies are downward shifts of the entire average cost function as experience is acquired.

Accordingly, policy support for expansion of the newcomers' share of the market is justified on economic grounds. In the context of renewable power, such policy support has taken the form of the direct and indirect subsidies noted above and, increasingly, RPS mandates at the state level.

Apart from the reality that the market for electric power is large, with several competing technologies, one central conceptual problem with the infant-industry argument is that many industries employing competing technologies display such characteristics; but market forces operating through the domestic and international capital markets provide investment capital in anticipation of future scale/learning cost savings and higher economic returns. Accordingly, the infant-industry argument is a non sequitur because the market can foresee the potential for scale and learning efficiencies. Unless renewable power production has difficulty attracting investment capital *for reasons other than expected profitability*— an assumption that little evidence supports—the infant-industry argument does not provide an efficiency rationale for policy favoritism toward renewable technologies. That the subsidies discussed above have not induced such investment on a scale sufficient to remove the need for RPS mandates is not consistent with the assumption that the infant nature of the renewables industry—if indeed it is accurate to describe it that way— is a central impediment to competitiveness of renewable technologies.[70] In any event, in order to examine the issue of whether significant learning efficiencies and/or scale economies characterize wind and solar generation, we would like to have wind and solar cost data over time and across project sizes. The pattern of average costs over time, controlling for the size of projects, should provide insights about the importance of learning efficiencies; if they are important, we should see a pattern of declining average costs.[71] The pattern of average costs across size classes

---

[70] For a different skeptical discussion of the infant-industry argument, see Michaels, supra, fn. 13, pp. 28–30.

[71] We control for the capacity (or size) of individual projects also because the issue is not merely whether, say, a large wind turbine exhibits lower average cost than a smaller one; instead, the issue is whether scale and/or learning efficiencies are present at the industry level—that is, whether an expansion of the industry systematically yields lower average costs. In this context, the issue of the higher costs attendant upon the use of increasingly unfavorable sites remains important, as noted above in the discussion of siting constraints and transmission costs. Learning and/or scale efficiencies, even if present, are likely to be offset at the industry level at least partially by higher site-related costs and may be offset fully or even more than fully.

TABLE 3-1
DoE CAPACITY-WEIGHTED AVERAGE WIND PROJECT COSTS
(THOUSANDS OF YEAR 2009 DOLLARS PER MW)

Year	Cost	Year	Cost
1984	4,800	1997	2,450
1985	3,600	1998	1,450
1986	n/a	1999	1,600
1987	2,000	2000	1,600
1988	n/a	2001	1,300
1989	2,500	2002	1,550
1990	2,850	2003	1,450
1991	n/a	2004	1,300
1992	n/a	2005	1,520
1993	n/a	2006	1,600
1994	1,700	2007	1,700
1995	1,725	2008	1,950
1996	1,500	2009	2,120

SOURCE: Department of Energy, "2009 Wind Technologies Market Report," August 2010, figure 27, at http://www1.eere.energy.gov/windandhydro/pdfs/2009_wind_technologies_market_report.pdf.
NOTE: n/a—no data available.

in a given time period should yield inferences about the importance of scale economies. For wind generation, the Department of Energy reports data on capacity-weighted average project cost per MW over time, beginning in the early 1980s. If learning effects are important, we should expect to find declining costs, although it is clear that these data do not control well for other factors, which may or may not cancel each other out. Moreover, the data for the 1980s represent very small samples of projects, so that the information provided by those observations is much more limited than is the case for the later years. Table 3-1 presents these data, derived as estimates from a figure in the source cited.[72] These data,

---

[72] The Department of Energy cautions that the cost estimates for individual projects vary in quality, so that "emphasis should be placed on overall trends in the data" rather than the estimate for any given project. See Department of Energy, "2009 Wind Technologies Market Report," August 2010, p. 45, figure 27, at http://www1.eere.energy.gov/windandhydro/pdfs/2009_wind_technologies_market_report.pdf.

while somewhat crude, show a rough pattern of declining average costs from the 1980s through about 2001 and then rising average costs through 2009.[73] Since the data shown in table 3-1 are weighted by capacity, they provide a rough indicator of the importance of learning efficiencies in wind generation: they show rising average costs per wind MW after 2000–2001, suggesting that further learning efficiencies no longer are available to be exploited, unless, perhaps, future technological advances are made.[74] These data do not support the infant-industry assumption that learning efficiencies remain important in the case of wind-generation investments, although it is possible that learning efficiencies still are available but have been exceeded by the higher costs imposed by the use of increasingly unfavorable sites. It is possible also that the introduction of such subsidies as investment tax credits and cash grants based on costs rather than electricity production has reduced incentives to minimize costs.

Table 3-2 presents Department of Energy data on average costs by project size for wind projects installed in the 2007–2009 period.

TABLE 3-2

DoE Installed Average Wind Project Costs, 2007–2009
(thousands of year 2009 dollars per MW)

Project Size (MW)	Cost
<5	2,700
5–20	1,800
20–50	1,900
50–100	1,950
100–200	2,050
>200	2,050

Source: Department of Energy, op. cit., fn. 72 above, at figure 28.

---

[73] The Department of Energy displays a computed polynomial trend line that is shaped much like a U-shaped average cost function, although it is not actually an average cost function in that it is a trend line over time rather than a relation between the output rate and average cost. The trend line unambiguously declines before the 2000–2001 period and rises thereafter. See DoE, op. cit., fn. 72 above.
[74] Such advances would not be surprising; but the same is true for conventional generation technologies, so that an assumption of further technological advances for renewables does not necessarily imply increasing competitiveness and does not provide a useful rationale for subsidies on the basis of an infant-industry assumption.

These data suggest that scale economies are important only for small wind projects, and that average costs either constant or slightly increasing characterize projects larger than about 20 MW or thereabouts.

Reliable time-series data on costs for photovoltaic and solar-thermal systems are more difficult to find in the literature; perhaps the only consistent series is provided by the EIA in the assumptions published each year for the *Annual Energy Outlook*.[75] Table 3-3 presents these data adjusted for inflation.

TABLE 3-3
FIXED COSTS FOR SOLAR-ELECTRIC CAPACITY
(THOUSANDS OF YEAR 2009 DOLLARS PER MW)

Year	Photovoltaic	Thermal
2000	5,386	3,679
2001	4,749	3,199
2002	4,744	3,194
2003	5,247	3,528
2004	5,211	3,504
2005	5,219	3,509
2006	5,220	3,510
2007	6,006	4,031
2008	6,239	5,236
2009	6,239	5,237

SOURCE: See fn. 75; and author computations.
NOTE: Photovoltaic is for 5 MW; thermal is for 100 MW. These EIA calculations are for capital and fixed operations and maintenance costs. They are intended to represent real resource costs—that is, excluding the effects of tax preferences.

Given that these estimates are per MW, the decline in costs for both photovoltaic and thermal systems early in the decade suggests the exploitation of learning efficiencies and, perhaps, the use of more suitable sites. The increase in costs per MW after 2002 may suggest that no further

---

[75] These can be found in the annual Electricity Market Module discussions contained within the "Assumptions" chapters, at http://www.eia.doe.gov/oiaf/archive.html, various years.

learning efficiencies are available to be exploited; that costs rise after 2002 suggests that the problem of rising site costs is significant. On the other hand, a different data analysis for photovoltaics only, published by the Department of Energy, shows a decline in the capacity-weighted average installed cost from $10.80 per watt (2008 dollars) in 1998 to $7.50 per watt in 2008.[76] In short, the data are mixed in the case of solar-generation systems; the infant-industry assumption of significant learning and/or scale economies as a barrier to adoption of the technologies is far from obviously correct.

Leveling the Playing Field

A second central argument made in favor of policy support for renewables is essentially a level-playing-field premise: Because conventional generation benefits from important tax preferences and other policy support, renewables cannot compete without similar interventions.[77] The Government Accountability Office in 2007 estimated that between FY2002 and FY2007 approximately $4.2 billion (in year 2007 dollars) in electricity-related federal R&D funding and tax expenditures went to renewables, while $23 billion went to nuclear technologies, fossil fuels, and electricity transmission.[78]

In order to examine the level-playing-field argument, we must disaggregate the subsidies and support per unit of weighted capacity or generation on average and, if possible, on the margin.[79] One comprehensive review

---

[76] See U.S. Department of Energy, "Solar Technologies Market Report," January 2010, figure 3.9, at http://www1.eere.energy.gov/solar/pdfs/46025.pdf.

[77] As an example, see the letter dated January 6, 2009, to the majority leaderships of the House and Senate from a number of trade associations and others, at http://www.seia.org/galleries/pdf/Renewable_Energy_Stimulus_Letter_1_7_09.pdf.

[78] See U.S. Government Accountability Office, "Federal Electricity Subsidies," GAO-08-102, October 2007, p. 18–30, at http://www.gao.gov/new.items/d08102.pdf.

[79] Other things held constant, subsidies that affect the marginal (or incremental) cost of generation or the per-unit prices received by producers are likely to affect market prices, even under standard rate-of-return regulation, and so might create a competitive disadvantage for other technologies not receiving equivalent treatment. An example is the per-unit production tax credit for renewable power noted above. Other credits might improve profitability without affecting marginal costs or prices directly; investment tax credits for renewables are a good example. The latter would attract additional investment into the industry over time, thus perhaps affecting market prices, but that price effect would be felt by all producers regardless of which actually received the subsidy. At the same time, even such subsidies as the latter would serve to reduce or eliminate whatever competitive disadvantages confront renewables as a result of policies favoring conventional generation.

of federal financial interventions and subsidies in energy markets in 2007 was published by the EIA[80]; tables 3-4 and 3-5 summarize those findings. Table 3-4 presents total subsidies by fuel type or end use.

TABLE 3-4

FY2007 ELECTRICITY-PRODUCTION SUBSIDIES AND SUPPORT (MILLIONS OF YEAR 2009 DOLLARS)

Fuel/End Use	Direct Outlays	Tax Exp.	R&D	Federal Elec. Support	Total
Coal (pulverized)	n/a	272	538	70	881
Refined coal	n/a	2,223	n/a	n/a	2,223
Nat. gas/pet. liq.	n/a	209	4	21	234
Nuclear	n/a	205	951	151	1,307
Renewables	3.1	747	111	178	1,039
Transmission/dist.	n/a	758	144	371	1,274
Total	3.1	4,415	1,749	791	6,957

SOURCES: EIA, supra, fn. 15, at p. 105, table 34; and author computations.
NOTE: Totals may not sum due to rounding. n/a—not applicable or negligible.

Table 3-5 presents the EIA data by fuel and end use per mWh. Only refined-coal generation received per-unit federal subsidies and support higher than those for solar and wind generation; since refined-coal generation was only about 3.6 percent of total coal generation in 2007, it is difficult to believe that those higher subsidies represent a competitive hindrance to the adoption of solar- or wind-generation technologies.[81] More to the point, the federal solar and wind subsidies are far higher than those enjoyed by fossil fuels, nuclear, or hydroelectric generation,

---

[80] See EIA, supra, fn. 15.

[81] Refined coal is lower-quality coal from which some moisture and pollutants have been removed and that upon combustion emits fewer pollutants because of enhanced heat content. Total coal-fired net electric generation in 2007 was about 2.02 million gWh, of which 1.95 million gWh was from traditional (pulverized) coal technology, while generation using refined coal was about 72,000 gWh.

TABLE 3-5
FY2007 ELECTRICITY-PRODUCTION
SUBSIDIES AND SUPPORT PER MWH
(YEAR 2009 DOLLARS)

Fuel/End Use	Dollars per mWh
Municipal solid waste	0.13
Natural gas, petroleum liquids	0.26
Coal (pulverized)	0.45
Hydroelectric	0.69
Biomass, biofuels	0.92
Geothermal	0.95
Landfill gas	1.41
Nuclear	1.64
Wind	24.10
Solar	25.10
Refined coal	30.74
Weighted average	1.70

SOURCES: EIA, supra, fn. 15, at p. 106, table 35; and author computations.

and these relative differentials have not changed appreciably in the last three years.

The relative magnitudes of the subsidies per mWh are highly suggestive, given that the solar and wind subsidies are two orders of magnitude greater than those received by coal and natural gas technologies. It appears clear that solar and wind technologies are not at a competitive disadvantage because of subsidies enjoyed by conventional generation; quite the reverse is true. At the same time, the calculations presented in table 3-5 are average subsidies per mWh. A more-direct calculation of marginal subsidies and support has been reported by Metcalf, yielding estimates of effective marginal tax rates on investments in alternative electric-generation technologies. Computation of such effective marginal tax rates incorporates the many subsidies and preferences that affect choices among those alternatives and so offers a direct test of the degree to which federal policies favor given technologies over others.[82] Table 3-6 summarizes his findings, which also are for 2007.

TABLE 3-6
METCALF FINDINGS ON EFFECTIVE MARGINAL TAX RATES
FOR ELECTRIC-GENERATION INVESTMENT
(PERCENT)

Technology Depreciation	Current Law	No Tax Credits	Economic
Coal (pulverized)	38.9	38.9	39.3
Gas	34.4	34.4	39.3
Nuclear	−99.5	32.4	−49.4
Solar thermal	−244.7	12.8	−26.5
Wind	−163.8	12.8	−13.7

SOURCE: Metcalf 2010, op. cit., fn. 82.
NOTE: Current law is as of 2007.

The three columns present the Metcalf calculations of effective marginal tax rates under current law (as of 2007), under a regime without production and investment tax credits, and with economic depreciation assumed in place of accelerated depreciation, respectively.[83] Under current law, solar-thermal and wind generation investments receive net percentage marginal subsidies (negative effective marginal tax rates) far larger than those enjoyed by nuclear investments; and coal and gas investments face effective tax rates greater than zero. If the tax credits are assumed away, solar-thermal and wind investments face effective tax rates roughly one-third those of the other technologies. If economic depreciation replaces accelerated depreciation, nuclear investment enjoys a negative effective

[82] See Gilbert E. Metcalf, "Investment in Energy Infrastructure and the Tax Code," in Jeffrey R. Brown, ed., *Tax Policy and the Economy, Volume 24* (Chicago: University of Chicago Press Journals, 2010), 1–33. See also Metcalf, "Federal Tax Policy Towards Energy," NBER working paper no. 12568, October 2006, at http://www.nber.org/papers/w12568.pdf; and Metcalf, "Taxing Energy in the United States: Which Fuels Does the Tax Code Favor?", Manhattan Institute Center for Energy Policy and the Environment, report no. 4, January 2009, at http://www.manhattan-institute.org/html/eper_04.htm.
[83] Metcalf uses an exponential depreciation rate rather than straight-line depreciation as an approximation of economic depreciation over the lives of given investments.

marginal tax rate (tax subsidy) larger (in absolute value) than those for solar and wind investments; but coal and gas investments face effective marginal tax rates of over 39 percent.

The Metcalf calculations of effective marginal tax rates under current law suggest strongly that the *offsetting-subsidy* rationale for public support for solar and wind investments is incorrect: coal and gas investments face positive effective marginal tax rates, and new nuclear investment no longer is a serious competitive threat.[84] Moreover, the effective subsidies enjoyed by solar and wind generation are far greater than those needed to level the playing field with respect to nuclear generation.[85]

Adverse External Effects of Conventional Generation

A negative *externality* is an adverse effect of economic activity the costs of which are not borne by the parties engaging directly in the activity yielding the adverse effect. A simple example is the emission of effluents into the air as a byproduct of such industrial processes as power generation.[86] If the direct and third parties—those emitting effluents and consuming the electricity and the third parties adversely affected—cannot negotiate a resolution of the problem (usually because negotiation among numerous parties is difficult), standard economic analysis prescribes a (normative) solution: It is efficient to impose emission standards or taxes or some other policy tool

---

[84] The last nuclear-generation reactor to begin operation is the Watts Bar-1 plant in Tennessee, which began commercial operation on May 27, 1996. See EIA, at http://www.eia.gov/cneaf/nuclear/page/operation/statoperation.html. However, the Tennessee Valley Authority has announced plans to complete Watts Bar-2.

[85] The playing field is biased in favor of renewables for two additional reasons, the first of which is the implicit subsidy for backup generation capacity and transmission costs: such costs are a direct effect of investment in renewable capacity but are spread across electricity consumption from all sources. See, supra, fn. 46. Second, public subsidies for renewable power, whether in the form of direct outlays or indirect tax preferences, impose costs upon the private sector larger than the subsidies themselves because of the excess burden (or *deadweight losses*) created by the tax system. Essentially, the private sector becomes smaller by more than a dollar when it is forced to send a dollar to the federal government. For a nontechnical discussion, see Martin A. Feldstein, "The Effect of Taxes on Efficiency and Growth," *Tax Notes*, May 8, 2006, pp. 679–684, at http://www.nber.org/feldstein/taxanalysis.pdf.

[86] Just as the polluter imposes costs upon others, the latter group, if given the right to constrain the behavior of the polluter, imposes costs upon the polluter. More generally, despite the intuitive appeal of the argument that the polluter is the source of the pollution problem, the actual cause is competition for the use of a scarce resource, in this case, the air.

so as to confront all parties—the emitters of effluents, the consumers of the electricity or other goods produced, and those harmed by the pollution—with the full costs of the economic interaction so that such economic choices as the amount of electricity to produce or to consume are shaped by an efficient set of perceived costs and prices.[87]

There is no dispute that power generation with fossil fuels imposes adverse environmental effects in the form of sulfur dioxide, nitrogen oxides, mercury, particulates, and other effluents.[88] Accordingly, the EPA and the states have established detailed programs for defining emission standards and for implementing attendant investment and enforcement programs.[89] Whether these regulatory policies have internalized the adverse external effects of conventional electricity generation efficiently (or fully) is a topic outside the scope of this discussion.[90]

---

[87] This does not mean that zero pollution would be efficient. Some pollution is worth what it costs—that is, the cost of reducing it further in terms of the value of goods and services forgone is greater than the incremental value of the improved environmental quality gained. For the classic discussion of this problem, see Ronald Coase, "The Problem of Social Cost," *Journal of Law & Economics* 3 (October 1960): 1–44, at http://www.jstor.org/pss/724810. One of Coase's essential points is that in cases in which high transaction costs prevent a negotiated resolution by the parties themselves, it is efficient to allocate property rights for the use of the resource (for example, the air) in dispute so as to minimize the sum of externality costs and externality-avoidance costs. In other words, efficient policy should seek to induce two kinds of actions: those that reduce pollution and those that mitigate the harmful effects of pollution. For a short discussion of why the "polluter pays" principle thus may be incorrect, see Benjamin Zycher, "Oil Producers' Liability Should Not Be Unlimited," Forbes.com, June 25, 2010, at http://www.forbes.com/2010/06/24/oil-spill-liability-economics-opinions-contributors-benjamin-zycher.html. See also Patrik Söderholm and Thomas Sundqvist, "Pricing Environmental Externalities in the Power Sector: Ethical Limits and Implications for Social Choice," *Ecological Economics* 46 (2003): 333–350.

[88] For a brief discussion, see EIA, "Assumptions to the Annual Energy Outlook 2010," at http://www.eia.doe.gov/oiaf/aeo/assumption/electricity.html, and tables 8.7, 8.8, 8.9, and 8.10 at http://www.eia.gov/oiaf/aeo/assumption/pdf/electricity_tbls.pdf. We set aside here the issue of carbon dioxide emissions and global warming (or "climate change"), given the increasingly uncertain nature of the scientific and economic analyses underlying policy proposals ostensibly directed at the purportedly adverse effects of greenhouse gas emissions. However, some of the analyses listed in table 3-7 below attempt to include such effects in estimates of externality costs. With respect to the very large uncertainties, see, for example, Patrick J. Michaels and Robert C. Balling Jr., *Climate of Extremes: Global Warming Science They Don't Want You to Know*, Washington D.C.: Cato Institute, 2009; Richard S. Lindzen and Yong-Sang Choi, "On the Determination of Climate Feedbacks from ERBE Data," *Geophysical Research Letters* 36 (August 26, 2009); A. W. Montford, *The Hockey Stick Illusion: Climategate and the Corruption of Science* (London: Stacey International, 2010); Roy W. Spencer, *The Great Global Warming Blunder: How Mother Nature Fooled the World's Top Climate Scientists* (New York: Encounter Books, 2010); and Sally C. Pipes and Benjamin Zycher, "Attorneys General Versus the EPA," Pacific Research Institute monograph, December 2003, at https://www.pacificresearch.org/publications/id.174/pub_detail.asp.

[89] An introduction to these regulations can be found at http://www.epa.gov/air/clearskies/basic.html.

[90] For a summary discussion of efficiency in such regulatory and tax policies, see Don Fullerton and Gilbert E. Metcalf, "Environmental Controls, Scarcity Rents, and Pre-existing Distortions," *Journal of Public Economics* 80, no. 2 (May 2001): 249–267.

If the negative externalities yielded by conventional generation are not internalized fully by current environmental policies, then the costs of conventional generation as perceived by the market would be (artificially) lower than the true social costs. This would create a separate dimension of the level-playing-field issue discussed above in the context of explicit and implicit subsidies. And so the question to be addressed is as follows: Given the magnitude of those externalities as estimated in the technical literature, are the additional (or marginal) costs of backup capacity imposed by renewable generation sufficient to offset any artificial cost advantage enjoyed by conventional generation? Several analyses of the externality costs of U.S. electricity generation were conducted during the 1980s and

TABLE 3-7

ESTIMATES OF EXTERNALITY COSTS
OF U.S. ELECTRICITY GENERATION
(YEAR 2009 CENTS PER KWH)

Study	Year	Coal	Gas	Oil	Nuclear	Hydro	Solar	Wind
				Generation Type				
Bernow et al.	1991	7.1–16.0	2.7–10.2	5.6–16.5				
Chernick, Caverhill	1989	5.6–9.9	2.2–3.4	6.2–10.1				
Cifuentes, Lave	1993	2.8–26.5	0.1					
Hall	1990				3.0–4.3			
Oak Ridge, RFF	1994–1996	0.1–0.6	0.01–0.04	0.05–0.4	0.03–0.2	0.03		
Ottinger et al.	1990	4.6–11.4	1.3–2.1	5.0–13.3	4.9	1.8–2.1	0–0.6	0–0.2
Putta	1991	2.2						
Rowe et al.	1996	0.4	0.3	0.9	0.01			0

SOURCES: See fn. 92; and author computations.

1990s.[91] These studies differ somewhat in terms of methodology and focus but offer a range of estimates useful in terms of the question addressed here. Table 3-7 summarizes the findings of this empirical literature.[92]

Note that the figures in table 3-7 are estimates of environmental externality costs only and do not include the additional costs of backup-generation capacity and transmission imposed by solar and wind investments. The estimated externality costs for coal range from 0.1 cents per kWh to 26.5 cents per kWh. For gas generation, the range is 0.1 to 10.2 cents per kWh. For oil, nuclear, and hydro generation, the respective

---

[91] The EIA published in 1995 a summary of case studies for several states, estimated in dollars per ton of effluent. See EIA, "Electricity Generation and Environmental Externalities: Case Studies," September 1995, at http://www.eia.doe.gov/cneaf/electricity/external/external.pdf. These estimates are not directly comparable with those summarized in table 3-7. Note that renewable-power generation imposes its own set of problems, including noise, light-flicker effects, deaths among possibly large numbers of birds, consumption of large amounts of land with unsightly turbine farms or solar-collection panels, and others. See also fns. 62 and 63, supra. Interestingly, new research finds that large-scale adoption of wind generation might cause an increase in surface temperatures. See C. Wang and R.G. Prinn, "Potential Climatic Impacts and Reliability of Very Large-Scale Wind Farms," *Atmospheric Chemistry and Physics* 10, no. 4 (2010): 2052–2061, at http://www.atmos-chem-phys.net/10/2053/ 2010/acp-10-2053-2010.pdf. A few summary reviews of the (older) literature are available: One is C. B. Szpunar, "Compendium of Selected References on Air Emissions; Health, Risk, and Valuation Research; and Environmental Externalities," Argonne National Laboratory, July 1992, at http://www.osti.gov/bridge/purl.cover.jsp;jsessionid=01F813A39517FD63EDA1C1C903E7D967?purl=/ 7181277-QIpyku/. Another is Office of Technology Assessment, "Studies of the Environmental Costs of Electricity," OTA-BP-ETI-134, September 1994, at http://www.fas.org/ota/reports/9433.pdf. See also Thomas Sundvist and Patrik Söderholm, "Valuing the Environmental Impacts of Electricity Generation: A Critical Survey," *Journal of Energy Literature* 8, no. 2 (December 2002): 3–41.

[92] See Stephen Bernow, Bruce Biewald, and Donald Marron, "Full-Cost Dispatch: Incorporating Environmental Externalities in Electric System Operation," *The Electricity Journal* 4, no. 2 (March 1991): 20–33; Paul Chernick and Emily Caverhill, "The Value of Externalities from Energy Production, Delivery, and Use: Fall 1989 Update," December 22, 1989, summarized in Office of Technology Assessment, op. cit., fn. 91; Luis A. Cifuentes and Lester B. Lave, "Economic Valuation of Air Pollution Abatement: Benefits From Health Effects," *Annual Review of Energy and the Environment* 18 (November 1993): 319–342; Darwin C. Hall, "Preliminary Estimates of Cumulative Private and External Costs of Energy," *Contemporary Policy Issues* 8, no. 3 (July 1990): 283–307; Oak Ridge National Laboratory and Resources for the Future, *Estimating Externalities of Fuel Cycles*, reports 2–8 (Washington D.C.: McGraw-Hill/Utility Data Institute, 1994–1996); Richard L. Ottinger et al., *Environmental Costs of Electricity*, Pace University Center for Environmental Legal Studies, 1990; Sury N. Putta, "Methods for Valuing and Incorporating Environmental Costs in Electric Resource Planning and Acquisition," in Olav Hohmeyer and Richard L. Ottinger, eds., *External Environmental Costs of Electric Power: Analysis and Internalization: Proceedings of a German American Workshop* (Berlin: Springer Verlag, 1991), 371–389; and Robert D. Rowe et al., *New York State Environmental Externalities Cost Study* (New York: Farrar, Straus, Giroux, 1996). See also Paul W. Parfomak, "Falling Generation Costs, Environmental Externalities, and the Economics of Electricity Conservation," *Energy Policy* 25, no. 10 (August 1997): 845–860. Note that some of the analyses estimate damage (for example, health) costs from effluents, while others estimate mitigation costs. In principle, those should be equal (on the margin) if environmental policy is efficient.

ranges are 0.4 to 16.5 cents per kWh, 0 to 4.9 cents per kWh, and 0 to 2.1 cents per kWh.

The highest estimated figure for coal generation is 26.5 cents per kWh, or $265 per mWh. From the discussion above of the cost of backup capacity, existing wind- and solar-generation investments have imposed a backup cost of about $368 per mWh, or roughly 37 cents per kWh. Accordingly, if all conventional generation were coal-fired, existing wind and solar capacity would impose a backup cost externality about 39 percent higher than the environmental externality costs of conventional generation under the implausible assumption that none of the conventional externalities have been internalized under current environmental policy. In addition, wind and solar capacity imposes extra transmission costs of about $5 to $6 per mWh (table 2-1) or more and enjoy additional subsidies well over $20 per mWh (table 3-5).

But in fact coal generation is a bit less than 45 percent of total U.S. generation; gas generation is about 23 percent, nuclear generation is about 20 percent, hydroelectric generation is about 7 percent, and renewables and other miscellaneous technologies make up the rest.[93] If we use those figures and the highest estimates by fuel type in table 3-7 to compute a weighted-average externality cost for nonrenewable generation, the externality cost per conventional kWh is about 15.5 cents, or $155 per mWh.[94] If we use instead the midpoints of the externality ranges listed above, the weighted average externality cost is 7.8 cents per kWh, or $78 per mWh. Relative to the backup cost externality (37 cents per kWh) imposed by wind and solar investments alone, those figures are sufficiently low to cast substantial doubt on the externality argument for renewables subsidies: current environmental regulation must internalize some substantial part of conventional externalities, and state subsidies, both explicit and implicit, and RPS standards also have the effect of offsetting any artificial cost advantage enjoyed by conventional generation as a result of uninternalized externalities.

Note that in terms of economic efficiency, subsidies for renewables intended to offset the (assumed) uninternalized external costs of conventional generation are a second-best policy at best. Such subsidies would

---

[93] See the EIA data for 2009, at http://www.eia.gov/cneaf/electricity/epm/table1_1.html.
[94] Computed as 26.5 (.446) + 10.2 (.233) + 16.5 (.01) + 4.9 (.202) + 2.1 (.069).

reduce the (inefficient) competitive advantage of conventional generation yielded by the presence of some social costs unreflected in prices; but they would not improve the efficiency of costs or prices for conventional generation. And by biasing the perceived costs and prices of renewable generation downward, the subsidies would result in a total electricity market that would be too large. In short, the externality argument in favor of policy support for renewable electricity generation is exceedingly weak, far more so than commonly assumed.

The Resource Depletion or "Sustainability" Argument

As noted at the outset, renewable energy has no uniform definition; but the (assumed) finite physical quantity of conventional energy sources is the essential characteristic differentiating the two in most discussions. This "self-replenishment" of sunlight and wind flows is the central characteristic of *sustainability*, perhaps a broader concept, which has been defined by the EPA as "the satisfaction of basic economic, social, and security needs now and in the future without undermining the natural-resource base and environmental quality on which life depends."[95]

In an economic sense, the energy content of sunlight and wind is finite: they contain only so much convertible energy, and they are not always available. Moreover, the same is true for the other resources—materials, land, etc.—on which the conversion of such renewable energy into electricity depends. One large problem with the EPA perspective just noted is that the interest of future generations is not consistent with a maximization of the future resource base.[96] Consider a homo sapiens born in a cave some tens of thousands of years ago, in a world with a resource base virtually undiminished and an environment effectively untouched by mankind. That child at birth would have had a life expectancy on the order of ten years; had it been able to choose, it is obvious that it willingly would have given up some resources and

---

[95] See the brief sustainability discussion from February 2011 at http://epa.gov/sustainability/basic info.htm.

[96] This is not a straw man. Unless we have a definition of "undermining the natural-resource base," we are left with the sense that a nontrivial reduction in the quantity of a given natural resource bequeathed to future generations would be viewed by them as an affront.

environmental quality in exchange for better housing, food, water, medical care, ad infinitum.[97] More generally, the central interest of future generations is the inheritance from previous generations of the largest possible capital stock, of which the resource base and environmental quality are two important dimensions among many. If artificially high "conservation" of resources by the current generation yields a smaller total capital stock for future generations, then some additional under-mining of the natural-resource base would be preferred (efficient) from the viewpoint of the future generations.[98]

In any event, the basic sustainability concept seems to be that without policy intervention, market forces will result in the depletion (or exhaus-tion) of a finite resource.[99] Accordingly, subsidies and other support for renewable power generation are justified as tools with which to slow such depletion and to hasten the development of technologies that would provide alternatives for future generations.

That argument is deeply problematic. There is no particular reason to believe that government as an institution has incentives to adopt a time horizon longer than that relevant for the private sector; indeed, one plausible argument is that the time horizon for many public officials is the next election. Of course, to say that a given official views the next election as the "long run" is different from arguing that government acting collec-tively would display the same behavior; but the profit motive provides incentives for the market to consider the long-run effects of current decisions, while no similar constraint operates in the public sector, except perhaps crudely through democratic processes. In addition, such policies

---

[97] The life-expectancy estimate is taken from a telephone discussion, February 16, 2011, with Professor Gail Kennedy, department of anthropology, University of California, Los Angeles. Note here the implicit normative assumption that the "interests" of any individual or group are those that they would define for themselves.

[98] The capital stock includes both tangible capital and such intangibles as the rule of law, the stock of knowledge, culture, and the like. Greater wealth for the current generation yielded by resource depletion can yield conditions allowing the expansion of such other dimensions of the capital stock defined broadly.

[99] Note that for most such resources, increasing marginal costs of discovery and production is the usual characteristic, as some reserves of, say, natural gas are cheaper to produce than others. It is reasonable to predict that the market would never exhaust a given resource literally, as the cost of producing the last unit would be higher than the value of doing so. This simple point will be ignored here, and instead we assume that the production of finite resources is costless.

as campaign-finance restrictions may have had the effect of weakening the constraints that the political parties can impose on officeholders. As the parties are institutions with some incentives to adopt time horizons longer than those of particular officeholders, the net effect may have been a tendency to discount the future effects of policies more heavily. At the same time, the corporation income tax—a government policy—yields incentives for much of the private sector to discount the future more heavily than otherwise would be the case, as investments must earn a higher expected before-tax return in order to yield the market rate of return after taxes.[100]

More important, the market rate of interest is a price that links the interests of generations present and future.[101] If a resource is being depleted, then its expected future price will rise, other things held constant. If that rate of price increase is greater than the market interest rate, then owners of the resource have incentives to reduce production today—by doing so they can sell the resource in the future and in effect earn a rate of return higher than the market rate of interest—thus raising prices today and reducing expected future prices. In equilibrium—again, other factors held constant—expected prices should rise at the market rate of interest.[102] Under market institutions, it is the market rate of interest—the marginal rate of time preference—that ties the interests of the current and future generations by making it profitable currently to conserve some considerable volume of exhaustible resources for future consumption.[103] Because of the market rate of interest—the market price

---

100 Accordingly, trees are harvested, oil is produced, etc., sooner than otherwise would be the case. For the classic presentation of this analysis, see Arnold C. Harberger, "The Incidence of the Corporation Income Tax," *Journal of Political Economy* 70, no. 3 (June 1962): 215–240.

101 The interest rate is the price of current consumption in terms of forgone future consumption.

102 In reality the long-run prices of most exhaustible natural resources have declined (after adjusting for inflation) in large part because of technological advances in discovery, production, and use.

103 Strictly speaking, it is not the price of the resource that should rise at the market rate of interest; instead, the total economic return to holding the resource for future use should equal the market rate of interest. That economic return includes expected price changes and capital gains, expected cost savings, and the like. For a more detailed discussion, see Richard L. Gordon, "The Case against Government Intervention in Energy Markets," Cato Institute policy analysis no. 628, December 1, 2008, at http://www.cato.org/pub_display.php?pub_id=9810. See also, for example, Richard L. Gordon, "A Reinterpretation of the Pure Theory of Exhaustion," *Journal of Political Economy* 75, no. 3 (June 1967): 274–286.

of current resource use in terms of the value of forgone future use—market forces will never allow the depletion of a given resource.[104]

Accordingly, the market has powerful incentives to conserve; that is, to shift the consumption of some resources into future periods. That is why, for example, not all crude oil was used up decades ago even though the market price of crude oil always was greater than zero; that is, using it would have yielded value. Accordingly, the sustainability argument for policy support for renewable electricity depends crucially on an assumption that the market conserves too little and that government has incentives to improve the allocation of exhaustible resources over time. That is a dual premise for which the underlying rationale is weak and with respect to which little evidence has been presented.

"Green Jobs": Renewable Power as a Source of Expanded Employment

A common argument in support of expanded renewable power posits that policies in support of that goal will yield complementary employment growth in renewables sectors and stronger demand in the labor market in the aggregate.[105] But that argument almost certainly is incorrect in both of its central components: first, that an expansion of "green" employment would be an economic benefit of policy support for renewable electricity and, second, that such policies indeed can be predicted to yield higher employment for the economy writ large.

The employment created by renewables policies actually would be an economic cost rather than a benefit for the economy as a whole. While

---

[104] Of course this depends on enforcement of clearly defined property rights in the resource. If such rights are weak or unenforced, the resource becomes subject to the standard "tragedy of the commons" problem, an example of which is overfishing in international waters, the product of which (fish) is owned by no one until the fish are caught.

[105] See, for example, President Obama, supra, fns. 5 and 6. See also Robert Pollin et al., "Green Recovery: A Program to Create Good Jobs and Start Building a Low-Carbon Economy," Political Economy Research Institute, University of Massachusetts–Amherst, September 2008, at http://www.peri.umass.edu/fileadmin/pdf/other_publication_types/peri_report.pdf; and testimony of Bracken Hendricks, "Green Recovery: Investing in Clean and Efficient Energy to Create Jobs and Stimulate the Economy," Center for American Progress Action Fund, before the Committee on Energy and Natural Resources, U.S. Senate, December 10, 2008, at http://www.americanprogressaction.org/issues/2008/pdf/green_recovery_testimony.pdf.

that perhaps is a counterintuitive argument, suppose that policy support for renewables (or for any other sector) had the effect of increasing the demand for high-quality steel. That clearly would be a benefit for steel producers, or, more broadly, for owners of inputs in steel production, including steel workers. But for the economy as a whole, the need for additional high-quality steel in an expanding renewable-power sector would be an economic cost, as that steel (or the resources used to produce it) would not be available for use in other sectors. Similarly, the creation of "green jobs" as a side effect of renewables policies is a benefit for the workers hired (or for those whose wages rise with increased market competition for their services). But for the economy as whole, that use of scarce labor is a cost because those workers no longer would be available for productive activity elsewhere.[106]

There is the further matter that an expansion of the renewable-electricity sector must mean a decline in some other sector(s), with an attendant reduction in resource use there; after all, resources in the aggregate are finite. If there exists substantial unemployment and if labor demand in renewables is not highly specialized, a short-run increase in total employment might result. But in the long run—not necessarily a long period of time—such industrial policies cannot *create* employment; they can only shift it among economic sectors.[107] In short, an expanding renewables sector must be accompanied by a decline in other sectors, whether relative or absolute, and creation of green jobs must be accompanied by destruction of jobs elsewhere. Even if an expanding renewables sector is more labor-intensive (per unit of output) than the sectors that would decline as a result, it remains the case that the employment expansion would be a cost for the economy as a whole, and that the aggregate result would be an economy smaller than otherwise would be the case unless the underlying public policies succeed at correcting some distortion in

---

[106] Considerable employment would be created if policies encouraged ditchdigging with shovels (or, for that matter, spoons) rather than heavy equipment. Such employment obviously would be laughable—that is, an obvious economic burden. There is no analytic difference between this (silly) example and the green-jobs rationale for renewables subsidies.

[107] In this context, the *long run* is a period of time sufficient to allow resources, including labor, to move across economic sectors in response to changes in relative prices, public policies, and other such parameters.

market resource allocation, as discussed above.[108] There is no particular reason to believe that the employment gained as a result of the (hypothetically) greater labor intensiveness of renewables systematically would be greater than the employment lost because of the decline of other sectors combined with the adverse employment effect of the smaller economy in the aggregate. Moreover, we ignore here the adverse employment effects of the explicit or implicit taxes that must be imposed to finance the expansion of renewable power.

Because renewable-electricity generation is more costly than conventional generation, policies driving a shift toward heavier reliance on the former would increase aggregate electricity costs, thus reducing electricity use below levels that would prevail otherwise. The 2007 EIA projection of total U.S. electricity consumption in 2030 was about 5.17 million gWh.[109] The latest EIA projection for 2030 is about 4.68 million gWh, a decline of about 9.5 percent.[110] The change presumably reflects some assumed combination of structural economic shifts, increased conservation, substitution of renewables for some conventional generation, and a price increase from about 8.8 cents per kWh to 9 cents (in 2009 dollars).[111] It would be surprising if that reduction failed to have some employment effect.

Figure 3-1 displays data on percent changes in real GDP, electricity consumption, and employment for the period 1970 through 2009.[112]

It is obvious from the aggregate trends that electricity use and labor employment are complements rather than substitutes; the simple correlation between the percent changes for the two is 0.61, meaning, crudely,

---

[108] Many advocates of renewables subsidies assert that the generation of solar and wind power is more labor intensive than conventional generation. See, for example, Pollin et al., op. cit., fn. 105, pp. 11–12. The assumption of greater labor intensity for renewable-power production is dubious: The operation of solar or wind facilities does not employ large amounts of labor, and it is far from clear that construction of solar or wind facilities is more labor intensive than construction of conventional generation facilities.

[109] See EIA, "Annual Energy Outlook 2007 with Projections to 2030," at http://www.eia.doe.gov/oiaf/archive/aeo07/aeoref_tab.html, at table 2. The btu/kWh conversion was made by the author at a rate of 3412 btu per kWh.

[110] See EIA, at http://www.eia.gov/forecasts/aeo/tables_ref.cfm, at table 8.

[111] See EIA, supra, fn. 109, at table 1; EIA, ibid.; and author computations.

[112] Sources: For real GDP, see Bureau of Economic Analysis, "Frequently Requested NIPA Tables," at http://www.bea.gov/national/nipaweb/SelectTable.asp?Popular=Y, and author computations; for civilian employment, see Bureau of Labor Statistics, "Household Data Annual Averages," at http://www.bls.gov/cps/cpsaat1.pdf; and for electricity retail sales, see EIA, at http://www.eia.doe.gov/emeu/aer/pdf/pages/sec8_5.pdf.

FIGURE 3-1

GDP, ELECTRICITY CONSUMPTION, EMPLOYMENT

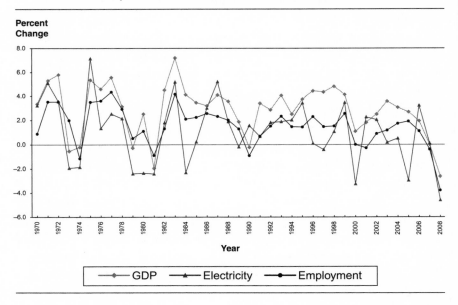

that a percent change in one tends to be observed with a 0.62 percent change in the other, in the same direction. The simple GDP/electricity and GDP/employment correlations are 0.67 and 0.85, respectively.

The correlations by themselves are not evidence of causation, the determination (or refutation) of which requires application (and statistical testing) of a conceptual model. But the data displayed in figure 3-1 make it reasonable to hypothesize that the higher costs and reduced electricity consumption attendant on expansion of renewable generation would reduce employment; and they clearly provide grounds to question the common assertion that policies in support of expanded renewable-electricity generation would yield increases in aggregate employment as a side effect.

It certainly is possible that the historical relationship between employ-ment and electricity consumption will change. Technological advances are certain to occur; but the prospective nature and effects of those shifts are difficult to predict.[113] The U.S. economy may evolve over time in ways yielding important changes in the relative sizes of industries and sectors; but, again, the direction of the attendant shifts in employment and electricity use is ambiguous.

But there exists no evidentiary basis on which to predict that a reduction in electricity consumption would yield an increase in employment. Like all geographic entities, the United States has certain long-term characteristics—climate, available resources, geographic location, trading partners, ad infinitum—that determine in substantial part the long-run comparative advantages of the economy in terms of economic activities and specialization. Figure 3-2 presents the historical paths of the electricity

FIGURE 3-2

ELECTRICITY CONSUMPTION RELATIONSHIPS

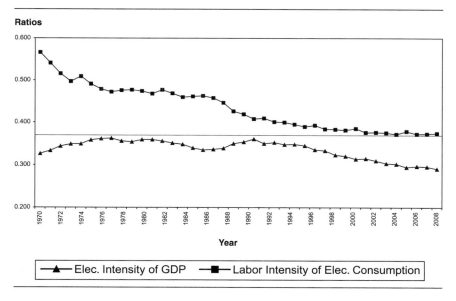

---

[113] Note that greater energy "efficiency" in any given activity can yield an increase in actual energy consumption if the elasticity of energy demand with respect to the marginal cost of energy use is greater than one. If, for example, air conditioning were to become sufficiently efficient in terms of energy consumption per degree of cooling, it is possible that air conditioners would be run so much that total energy consumption in space cooling would increase. A tax, on the other hand, whether explicit or implicit, increases the price of energy use and so unambiguously reduces energy consumption.

intensity of U.S. gross domestic product (GDP) (kWh per dollar of output) and of the labor intensity of U.S. electricity consumption (employment per kWh).

From 1970 to 2009, the electricity intensity of GDP increased and declined over various years but for the whole period has declined slightly at a compound annual rate of about 0.3 percent.[114] The labor intensity of U.S. electricity consumption—in a sense, the employment supported by each increment of electricity consumption—has declined more or less monotonically over the entire period at an annual compound rate of about 1.05 percent.[115] This may be the result largely of changes in the composition of GDP and perhaps the substantial increase in U.S. labor productivity in manufacturing; but these data do not suggest that a reduction in electricity consumption would yield an increase in aggregate employment. In short, while the employment/electricity relationship may have declined over time, there is no evidence that it is unimportant in an absolute sense.

Even given RPS mandates and other policy support for renewable technologies, it remains the case that they must compete with conventional technologies in terms of investment choices and market shares. One crucial dimension of such competition is the price of conventional fuels; chapter 4 discusses the implications of ongoing developments in the natural gas market.

---

[114] The electricity intensity of GDP was 0.326 in 1970 and 0.290 in 2009.
[115] The labor intensity of electricity consumption was 0.057 in 1970 and 0.037 in 2009. These data in figure 3-2 were scaled upward by a factor of ten for ease in presentation.

4

Some Implications of the Outlook for the Natural Gas Market

Recent technological advances in the production of natural gas from shale formations and from coal beds have increased estimated natural gas reserves sharply.[116] As a result, the EIA has increased its projections of future natural gas reserves and reduced its projections of future prices of natural gas delivered for electric generation.[117] Table 4-1 presents the EIA projections for natural gas reserves and prices published in the *Annual Energy Outlook* for 2010 and 2011.

TABLE 4-1
EIA NATURAL GAS PROJECTIONS

Year	AEO 2010	AEO 2011	AEO 2010	AEO 2011
	——Reserves——		——Prices——	
2015	254.61	279.40	6.24	4.79
2020	260.13	293.61	6.59	5.13
2025	259.77	299.51	6.94	5.91
2030	263.33	308.52	7.94	6.36
2035	267.94	314.16	8.69	6.97

SOURCE: Fn. 117 and author computations. EIA projections are reference cases.
NOTES: Reserves are dry natural gas in trillion cubic feet for the lower forty-eight states. Prices are in year 2009 dollars per thousand cubic feet delivered for electricity generation.

---

[116] For a brief discussion, see EIA, "What Is Shale Gas and Why Is It Important?" at http://www.eia.gov/energy_in_brief/about_shale_gas.cfm. See also, for example, Colorado School of Mines, *Potential Supply of Natural Gas in the United States*, December 31, 2008, summarized at http://www.mines.edu/Potential-Gas-Committee-reports-unprecedented-increase-in-magnitude-of-U.S.-natural-gas-resource-base.
[117] For EIA projections published in *Annual Energy Outlook 2010*, see EIA, at http://www.eia.gov/oiaf/archive/aeo10/aeoref_tab.html, at tables 13 and 14. For the projections published in *Annual Energy Outlook 2011* (early edition), see EIA, at http://www.eia.gov/forecasts/aeo/tables_ref.cfm, at tables 13 and 14.

Reserves projected in the 2011 publication are about 10–15 percent higher than those projected a year earlier through 2025 and then are about 17 percent higher for 2030 and 2035. Between the two sets of projections, prices fall by about 15 to 23 percent. Figure 4-1 illustrates the sharp increase over the last year or two in projected gas reserves that has resulted from the revolution in production technology for gas from shale and coal beds.[118] For any given future year, changes in projected reserves are small or negative in the *Annual Energy Outlook* editions for 2006 through 2009. But the change in projected reserves in the 2010 and 2011 editions are very large, reflecting the substantial shift in market conditions for natural gas attendant on these recent technological advances.

FIGURE 4-1

EIA PROJECTIONS: NATURAL GAS RESERVES

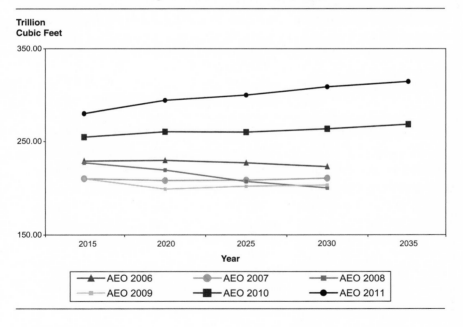

---

[118] These are the EIA projections for dry gas in the lower forty-eight states for 2015, 2020, 2025, 2030, and 2035 (2010 and 2011 editions), published in each *Annual Energy Outlook* for 2006, 2007, 2008, 2009, 2010, and 2011 (early edition). The intervening years are interpolated. See the various tables at http://www.eia.doe.gov/oiaf/archive.html.

TABLE 4-2
EIA PROJECTIONS OF ELECTRIC-GENERATING CAPACITY
(GIGAWATTS)

Year	AEO 2010 — Combined cycle gas —	AEO 2011	AEO 2010 — Non-hydro renewable —	AEO 2011
2015	168.5	170.7	76.0	57.7
2020	168.5	170.9	76.2	58.6
2025	175.2	177.2	78.3	63.1
2030	201.1	202.7	81.5	66.9
2035	211.6	226.8	89.8	69.9

SOURCES: Fn. 120 and author computations.

Table 4-2 shows the EIA projections for combined cycle gas-generation capacity and non-hydroelectric renewable generation capacity,[119] also published in the *Annual Energy Outlook* for 2010 and 2011.[120]

Combined cycle gas capacity in the two projections remains roughly the same until 2035, when the 2011 projection is about 7 percent higher than that made a year earlier. But the projections for non-hydroelectric renewable capacity fall by about 18 to 24 percent over the course of only one year.

These EIA projections of capacity investment in substantial part reflect the fact that gas and renewable generation technologies are substitutes and the projected decline in delivered gas prices increases the competitive disadvantages borne by renewable technologies, as discussed in chapter 2. Another way to approach this analytic issue is to make a rough estimate of the effect of cost changes affecting one technology upon investment in the other.[121] For natural gas power generation, gas costs are, conservatively,

---

[119] The EIA projection for renewables capacity includes hydroelectric and non-hydroelectric capacity. We assume constant hydroelectric capacity at 78 GW throughout the period and net that out to arrive at the figures for non-hydroelectric renewable capacity in table 4-2.

[120] For the capacity projections in *Annual Energy Outlook 2010*, see http://www.eia.gov/oiaf/archive/aeo10/aeoref_tab.html, at table 9. For the capacity projections in *Annual Energy Outlook 2011* (early edition), see http://www.eia.gov/forecasts/aeo/tables_ref.cfm, table 9.

[121] In economic terminology, this is the *cross-elasticity of demand* between investment in gas and renewable technologies—that is, the percent change in investment in one caused by a 1 percent change in the cost of the other.

half of total operating costs.[122] From table 2-1 we see that half of gas operations and maintenance cost would be about one-third of total cost (including fixed costs). Since our focus is on shifts in investment between gas and renewable generation technology, the question is what cross-elasticity of demand between the two alternative investments would have to be assumed to rationalize the changes in EIA capacity projections made in the 2010 and 2011 editions of the *Annual Energy Outlook*. From table 4-1, we see that the projected decline in delivered natural gas prices is about 15 to 23 percent; conservatively, this implies a decline in long-run gas-generation costs of about 5 to 8 percent. The decline in projected non-hydroelectric renewable capacity is about 18 to 24 percent.

This implies a cross-elasticity of demand for renewable-capacity investment with respect to the cost of gas generation of approximately three. Since an investment shift from a given renewable project to a gas project is straightforward in the long run, and that the electricity flows produced from the two alternatives are almost perfect substitutes, that crude estimate is wholly reasonable; indeed it may be conservative.[123] In short, the ongoing revolution in prospective natural gas supplies and the resulting long-run decline in relative natural gas prices are very likely to reduce the competitive position of wind and solar (and other renewable) electric-generation technologies even more than is already the case.

---

[122] Telephone interview, December 8, 2010, with Mr. Larry D. Hamlin, vice president for Power Production (retired), Southern California Edison Company, and California Energy Construction czar, February–April 2001. See also Andreas Back, "Lifecycle Costs and Investment," *Industrial Fuels and Power*, November 5, 2010, at http://www.ifandp.com/article/007997.html.

[123] Berndt and Wood find cross-elasticities of demand between energy and nonenergy inputs in U.S. industry of far less than one (in absolute value). Since energy and nonenergy inputs are certain to be less substitutable than conventional and renewable electricity, the fact that our crude estimate is an order of magnitude larger is reasonable. See Ernst R. Berndt and David O. Wood, "Technology, Prices, and the Derived Demand For Energy," *Review of Economics and Statistics* 57, no. 3 (August 1975): 259–268.

Conclusion

As a crude generalization, the experience in Europe in the context of renewable electricity can be summarized as high costs combined with low reliability.[124] That is the U.S. experience as well, an outcome unavoidable given the basic economic realities afflicting wind- and solar-power electric-generating technologies. Accordingly, renewable power generation has achieved only a small market share in the United States, and official projections are for slow growth at best, notwithstanding large subsidies and other policy support.

This market resistance to investment in renewable-generation capacity can be explained by the problems intrinsic to renewable power—that is, the inherent limitations on its competitiveness—that public policies can circumvent or neutralize only at very substantial cost. Those problems can be summarized as

- unconcentrated energy content,

- siting constraints and resulting high costs for transmission, and

- the costs created by low capacity factors, the intermittent nature of wind flows and sunlight, and the resulting need for backup capacity.

---

[124] See Kenneth P. Green, "The Myth of Green Energy Jobs: The European Experience," American Enterprise Institute, Energy and Environment Outlook no. 1 (February 2011), at http://www.aei.org/docLib/EEO-2011-02-No-2-g.pdf. See also Kenneth P. Green, "On Green Energy: A Dutch (Re)Treat," *The American* (April 10, 2011), at http://www.american.com/archive/2011/april/on-green-energy-a-dutch-re-treat. For an analysis of capacity factors for U.K. wind generation even lower than expected, see *Analysis of U.K. Wind Power Generation: November 2008 to December 2010*, John Muir Trust, March 2011, at http://www.jmt.org/assets/pdf/wind-report.pdf.

Moreover, the central analytic arguments that dominate the political and policy support for renewables are highly problematic: (1) The infant-industry argument is inconsistent with the cost evidence on renewables. (2) The subsidies enjoyed by renewables outweigh by far those bestowed on conventional-generation technologies. (3) The costs of backup capacity made necessary by renewable power—an externality that renewable power imposes on the electric system writ large—are greater than any negative externalities created by conventional generation and assumed not to have been corrected by current policies. (4) And the sustainability and green-employment rationales are exceedingly weak.

These realities suggest that the purported social benefits of policy support for renewables are illusory. Moreover, ongoing supply and price developments in the market for natural gas are likely to further weaken the competitive position of renewable-power generation. At the same time, the subsidies and mandates that have been implemented in support of renewable electricity impose nontrivial costs on the taxpayers and on consumers in electricity markets. The upshot is the imposition of sub-stantial net costs on the U.S. economy as a whole even as the policies bestow important benefits on particular groups and industries, thus yielding enhanced incentives for innumerable interests to seek favors from government. As has proven to be the case in most contexts, the out-comes of market competition, even as constrained and distorted by tax and regulatory policies, are the best guides for the achievement of resource allocation that is most productive. As federal and state policy-makers address the ongoing issues and problems afflicting renewable electricity generation, the realities of this recent history provide a useful guide for policy reform.

Index

About the Author

Benjamin Zycher is a visiting scholar at the American Enterprise Institute, a senior fellow at the Pacific Research Institute, and an associate in the Intelligence Community Associates program of the Office of Economic Research, Bureau of Intelligence and Research, U.S. Department of State. He is also a member of the advisory board of the quarterly journal *Regulation*.

He is a former senior fellow at the Manhattan Institute for Policy Research, a former senior economist at the RAND Corporation, a former member of the Board of Directors of the Western Economic Association International, a former adjunct professor of economics at the University of California, Los Angeles (UCLA), a former adjunct professor of economics and business at the California State University, Channel Islands, a former vice president for research at the Milken Institute, the founding editor of the quarterly public policy journal *Jobs & Capital*, a former senior staff economist at the President's Council of Economic Advisers, and a former member of the advisory board of *Consumer Alert*.

He holds a Ph.D. in economics from UCLA and a master's degree in public policy from the University of California, Berkeley. Among his publications are "Defense Economics" and "OPEC" in *The Concise Encyclopedia of Economics* (2008).

Board of Trustees

Kevin B. Rollins, *Chairman*
Senior Adviser
TPG Capital

Tully M. Friedman,
Vice Chairman
Chairman and CEO
Friedman Fleischer & Lowe, LLC

Gordon M. Binder
Managing Director
Coastview Capital, LLC

Arthur C. Brooks
President
American Enterprise Institute

The Honorable
Richard B. Cheney

Harlan Crow
Chairman and CEO
Crow Holdings

Daniel A. D'Aniello
Cofounder and Managing Director
The Carlyle Group

John V. Faraci
Chairman and CEO
International Paper Company

Christopher B. Galvin
Chairman
Harrison Street Capital, LLC

Raymond V. Gilmartin
Harvard Business School

Harvey Golub
Chairman and CEO, Retired
American Express Company

Robert F. Greenhill
Founder and Chairman
Greenhill & Co., Inc.

Frank J. Hanna
Hanna Capital, LLC

Bruce Kovner
Chairman
Caxton Associates, LP

Marc S. Lipschultz
Partner
Kohlberg Kravis Roberts & Co.

John A. Luke Jr.
Chairman and CEO
MeadWestvaco Corporation

Robert A. Pritzker
President and CEO
Colson Associates, Inc.

J. Peter Ricketts
President and Director
Platte Institute for Economic
 Research, Inc.

Edward B. Rust Jr.
Chairman and CEO
State Farm Insurance Companies

D. Gideon Searle
Managing Partner
The Serafin Group, LLC

The American Enterprise Institute
for Public Policy Research

Founded in 1943, AEI is a nonpartisan, nonprofit research
and educational organization based in Washington, DC.
The Institute sponsors research, conducts seminars and
conferences, and publishes books and periodicals.

AEI's research is carried out under three major programs: Economic Policy Studies, Foreign Policy and
Defense Studies, and Social and Political Studies. The
resident scholars and fellows listed in these pages are part
of a network that also includes adjunct scholars at leading
universities throughout the United States and in several
foreign countries.

The views expressed in AEI publications are those of
the authors and do not necessarily reflect the views of
the staff, advisory panels, officers, or trustees.

Mel Sembler
Founder and Chairman
The Sembler Company

Wilson H. Taylor
Chairman Emeritus
CIGNA Corporation

William H. Walton
Managing Member
Rockpoint Group, LLC

William L. Walton
Rappahannock Ventures, LLC

Marilyn Ware
Ware Family Office

James Q. Wilson
Boston College and
Pepperdine University

Emeritus Trustees

Willard C. Butcher

Richard B. Madden

Robert H. Malott

Paul W. McCracken

Paul F. Oreffice

Henry Wendt

Officers

Arthur C. Brooks
President

David Gerson
Executive Vice President

Jason Bertsch
Vice President, Development

Henry Olsen
Vice President; Director,
 National Research Initiative

Danielle Pletka
Vice President, Foreign and
 Defense Policy Studies

Council of Academic
Advisers

James Q. Wilson, *Chairman*
Boston College and
Pepperdine University

Alan J. Auerbach
Robert D. Burch Professor of
 Economics and Law
University of California, Berkeley

Eliot A. Cohen
Paul H. Nitze School of Advanced
 International Studies
Johns Hopkins University

Martin Feldstein
George F. Baker Professor
 of Economics
Harvard University

Robert P. George
McCormick Professor of Jurisprudence
Director, James Madison Program
 in American Ideals and Institutions
Princeton University

Gertrude Himmelfarb
Distinguished Professor of History
 Emeritus
City University of New York

R. Glenn Hubbard
Dean and Russell L. Carson Professor
 of Finance and Economics
Columbia Business School

John L. Palmer
University Professor and
 Dean Emeritus
Maxwell School of Citizenship
 and Public Affairs
Syracuse University

Sam Peltzman
Ralph and Dorothy Keller
 Distinguished Service Professor
 of Economics
Booth School of Business
University of Chicago

George L. Priest
John M. Olin Professor of Law
 and Economics
Yale Law School

Jeremy A. Rabkin
Professor of Law
George Mason University
School of Law

Richard J. Zeckhauser
Frank Plumpton Ramsey Professor
of Political Economy
Kennedy School of Government
Harvard University

Research Staff

Ali Alfoneh
Resident Fellow

Joseph Antos
Wilson H. Taylor Scholar in Health
Care and Retirement Policy

Leon Aron
Resident Scholar; Director,
Russian Studies

Paul S. Atkins
Visiting Scholar

Michael Auslin
Resident Scholar

Claude Barfield
Resident Scholar

Michael Barone
Resident Fellow

Roger Bate
Legatum Fellow in Global Prosperity

Walter Berns
Resident Scholar

Andrew G. Biggs
Resident Scholar

Edward Blum
Visiting Fellow

Dan Blumenthal
Resident Fellow

John R. Bolton
Senior Fellow

Karlyn Bowman
Senior Fellow

Alex Brill
Research Fellow

Charles W. Calomiris
Visiting Scholar

Lynne V. Cheney
Senior Fellow

Steven J. Davis
Visiting Scholar

Mauro De Lorenzo
Visiting Fellow

Christopher DeMuth
D. C. Searle Senior Fellow

Sadanand Dhume
Resident Fellow

Thomas Donnelly
Resident Fellow; Director,
AEI Center for Defense Studies

Nicholas Eberstadt
Henry Wendt Scholar in
Political Economy

Jon Entine
Visiting Fellow

Jonah Goldberg
Visiting Fellow

Scott Gottlieb, M.D.
Resident Fellow

Kenneth P. Green
Resident Scholar

Michael S. Greve
John G. Searle Scholar

Kevin A. Hassett
Senior Fellow; Director,
Economic Policy Studies

Steven F. Hayward
F. K. Weyerhaeuser Fellow

Robert B. Helms
Resident Scholar

Arthur Herman
NRI Visiting Scholar

Frederick M. Hess
Resident Scholar; Director,
Education Policy Studies

Ayaan Hirsi Ali
Resident Fellow

R. Glenn Hubbard
Visiting Scholar

Frederick W. Kagan
Resident Scholar; Director,
AEI Critical Threats Project

Leon R. Kass, M.D.
Madden-Jewett Chair

Karthik Kalyanaraman
NRI Fellow

Andrew P. Kelly
Research Fellow

Desmond Lachman
Resident Fellow

Adam Lerrick
Visiting Scholar

Philip I. Levy
Resident Scholar

Lawrence B. Lindsey
Visiting Scholar

John H. Makin
Resident Scholar

Aparna Mathur
Resident Scholar

Lawrence M. Mead
Visiting Scholar

Allan H. Meltzer
Visiting Scholar

Thomas P. Miller
Resident Fellow

Charles Murray
W. H. Brady Scholar

Roger F. Noriega
Visiting Fellow

Norman J. Ornstein
Resident Scholar

Pia Orrenius
Visiting Scholar

Richard Perle
Resident Fellow

Mark J. Perry
Visiting Scholar

Tomas J. Philipson
Visiting Scholar

Edward Pinto
Resident Fellow

Alex J. Pollock
Resident Fellow

Vincent R. Reinhart
Resident Scholar

Richard Rogerson
Visiting Scholar

Michael Rubin
Resident Scholar

Sally Satel, M.D.
Resident Scholar

Gary J. Schmitt
Resident Scholar; Director,
Program on American Citizenship

Mark Schneider
Visiting Scholar

David Schoenbrod
Visiting Scholar

Nick Schulz
DeWitt Wallace Fellow;
Editor-in-Chief, American.com

Roger Scruton
Visiting Scholar

Apoorva Shah
Research Fellow

Kent Smetters
Visiting Scholar

Christina Hoff Sommers
Resident Scholar; Director,
W. H. Brady Program

Phillip Swagel
Visiting Scholar

Erin Syron
NRI Fellow

Marc A. Thiessen
Visiting Fellow

Bill Thomas
Visiting Fellow

Alan D. Viard
Resident Scholar

Peter J. Wallison
Arthur F. Burns Fellow in
Financial Policy Studies

David A. Weisbach
Visiting Scholar

Paul Wolfowitz
Visiting Scholar

John Yoo
Visiting Scholar

Benjamin Zycher
NRI Visiting Fellow